Ethlyn Ottley Farrell

Prayers That Touch Heaven and Change Earth

2016

Scripture verses depicting KJV, NASB, AMP and NLT are taken from the The Comparative Study Bible, © 1994 by Zondervan Corporation, Grand Rapids, Michigan 49506, USA New Living Translation © 1996 by Tyndale Charitable Trust

Prayers That Touch Heaven *and* Change Earth

Copyright © 2016 by Ethlyn Ottley Farrell
Etty Farrell farrelle3@aol.com

ISBN 978-0-9977029-7-2
Library of Congress Control Number 2016955130

Published by Rapier Publishing Company
260 W. Main Street, Suite #1
Dothan, Alabama 36301
www.rapierpublishing.com

All rights reserved under the International Copyright Law. No part of this publication, to include may be reproduced, stored in a retrieval system, or transmitted in any form or by any means electronic, mechanical, photocopy, or any other means without the prior permission of the publisher or author except for brief quotations embodied in reviews and articles as they relate to the book.

First Edition
Printed in the United States of America.
For Information write to: Ethlyn O. Farrell P.O. Box #11893, St. Thomas, U.S.V.I., 00801 elynfarrell1987@gmail.com
Book Cover Design: Garrett Myers at garrettmyersart@gmail.com
Book Layout: Rapture Graphics.

The views expressed in this work are solely those of the author and do not necessarily reflect the views of the publisher, and the publisher hereby disclaims any responsibility for them.

Dedication

This book is dedicated to all those who are Intercessors around the world,
those who desire to learn to pray and for those who are weary of their assignment of prayer.
Be encouraged to stay on the wall, on task and in prayer for our breakthrough is eminent.
1 Thessalonians 5: 17
Pray without Ceasing

Acknowledgements

First and foremost I want to give all praise, glory, thanks and honor to my Lord and Savior, Jesus Christ, who has chosen me as a vessel to bring forth this project into the earth for such a time as this.

To my Diva Sisters, Michelle Smith Roberts and Michelle Mardenborough, thanks for your encouragement, prayers, love and support.

To the Intercessors of Victory In Prayer Center, Camela Francis, Jerry Todman, Norma Drayton, Michelle Mardenborough and Michelle Smith Roberts, a resounding thank you, for your commitment to the cause, your faithfulness to God in prayer and your prayers for me, my family and ministries.

To Prophet Dwayne, Senior Pastor Keri Fraser and the Abundant Rain Empowerment Church family, thanks for your love, support and every ministry opportunity.

Thanks to Beverly Petrus and Kim Industrious Ayala for your commitment to our daily prayer workouts, encouragement and support of my many projects and events.

To Apostle H.L. Smith, of Pentecostal Deliverance Ministries Fellowship International, Inc., thanks you for your wisdom and help with my ministry.

To Minister Elois Humphreys, the founder and president of Women in Position Ministry, thank you for your many words of encouragement, wisdom, ministry and business ideas to keep me on assignment.

To Pastor Carl and Dr. Reva Richardson of Living Hope Cathedral, thanks for your love and support.

To James Richardson, thank you for your tireless technical work, helpfulness, patience and kindness to me as I did this project.

To Shanelle Baron thank you for being available to help

wherever necessary.

Thanks to Fannie Pierce and Rapier Publishing for being confident of the gift of God on the inside of me and polishing it as it came forth on the outside.

To my many friends and family members, thank you for your continuous love, faithfulness, commitment and support.

In humble gratitude and with great appreciation to everyone, THANK YOU!

Foreword by Dr. Keri Fraser

Divine power and authority were demonstrated in the life and ministry of Jesus Christ as He introduced the Kingdom of God on earth. Sickness was no match for His healing, bondage was no match for His deliverance, poverty was no match for His riches, death was no match for His resurrection power and sin was no match for His saving grace. While the public ministry of Jesus Christ was indeed impressive, the secret to His successful ministry was His commitment to prayer. Through prayer, Jesus was enlightened and empowered to do great works. This commitment to prayer did not go unnoticed by His disciples. As a matter of fact, the disciples knew that if they wanted to walk in the same power and authority of Jesus, they would have to adopt his lifestyle of prayer. This desire prompted them to make a simple, yet life-changing request, "Lord, teach us to pray."

Prayer is an essential and effective tool for believers. It is critical if we expect the will of God to be done in earth as it is in heaven. Our prayers are effective when we follow the pattern God has outlined. God watches over His word to perform it. If we pray the Word of God, then we have the guarantee that God will in fact watch over our prayer and whatever we ask in His name shall be done.

"Prayers that Touch Heaven and Change Earth," is a remarkable tool which will propel your prayer life to another level. It will take you to higher heights and deeper depths in God. This book is exactly what the Body of Christ needs in this hour to fight the good fight of faith. Minister Ethlyn Farrell has provided a collection of strategic prayers which serves as a powerful guide for those who desire to make a greater impact in the earth. We are in a season of signs, wonders and miracles, but they must be birthed through the ministry of prayer.

Minister Ethlyn Farrell serves as an anointed intercessor in the Body of Christ. The success of her life and ministry is the result of the discipline in her prayer closet. I have personally witnessed her commitment to praying Word-based, Faith-driven, Power-packed prayers in her own life for many years. I am excited that she has been led by God to share these prayers with other believers. Your prayer life will never be the same once you apply the principles revealed in this book. Get ready to experience the Kingdom, Power and Glory of God in the earth. God will position you to make an impact as you touch Heaven and change Earth through your fervent prayers.

Dr. Keri Fraser Senior Pastor
Abundant Rain Empowerment Church
Decatur, Georgia

Table of Contents

- Prayer Book: Introduction..............................13
- Why We Pray...17
- The Essentials to Effective Prayer................19
- The Essentials to Effective Prayer Are:.........21
- Types of Prayer..23
- Prayer for the Government...........................26
- Praying for Our Church Leaders..................29
- Prayers for Marriage: Husbands & Wives.......31
- Prayer for Marriage 34
- Intimacy in Marriage....................................36
- Surviving Divorce...37
- Prayer for Children.......................................39
- Prayer for our School Systems......................42
- Prayer for families going through Separation and Divorce...43
- Prayer for Forgiving Yourself and Others...45
- Prayer for Rededication for Backslidden Believers..46
- Prayer of Thanksgiving.................................47
- Prayer for Direction.....................................49
- Praying for Wisdom......................................50
- Renewing the Mind......................................51
- Salvation..52
- Salvation for the Lost...................................53
- Gathering the End time Harvest...................54
- Greater Works 55
- Having Love One for Another......................57
- Ministry..58
- The Five-Fold Ministry.................................61
- Provision for the Vision...............................63

BUSINESS	65
FINANCES	67
KNOWING GOD AS OUR SOURCE	68
UNDERSTANDING THE GRACE OF GOD	69
SINGLES LOOKING FOR A MATE	71
SINGLE AND SATISFIED	73
STRENGTH TO STAND IN ADVERSITY	74
TRAVELING MERCIES	76
PREPARING FOR SURGERY	77
WALKING INTO VICTORY	78
MEN AFFIRMING MEN	79
WARFARE PRAYER	81
WARFARE PRAYER FOR THE FIVE-FOLD MINISTRY: APOSTLES, PROPHETS, EVANGELISTS, PASTORS AND TEACHERS	82
WARFARE PRAYER FOR GENERATIONAL CONTROLLING SPIRITS	84
WARFARE PRAYER FOR EMOTIONAL DISTRESS	86
WARRING AGAINST WRONG ATTITUDES	88
WARFARE PRAYER FOR CHILDREN	90
PRAYER AGAINST HUMAN TRAFFICKING	92
HEALING	94
HEALING FOR VICTIMS OF INCEST	96
HEALING FOR VICTIMS OF RAPE	98
HEALING FOR VICTIMS OF MOLESTATION	100
HEALING FOR MEN WHO GREW UP WITHOUT A FATHER	101
HEALING FOR THOSE STRUGGLING WITH THEIR SEXUAL IDENTITY	102
HEALING FOR THE BROKEN HEART	104
HEALING FOR CHILDREN REJECTED BY PARENTS	105
CHILDBEARING DIFFICULTY CONCEIVING BARRENNESS	106

SHIFTING THE ATMOSPHERE	108
PRAYER FOR ISRAEL	110
PRAYER FOR PEACE IN THE COUNTRIES OF THE WORLD	111
PRAYER FOR INTERCESSORS AND PRAYER WARRIORS	113
SCRIPTURAL GLOSSARY	115
THE ALPHA AND OMEGA OF PRAYER	127

Prayers That Touch Heaven And Change Earth

Prayer Book: Introduction

Over the years as a believer, I heard it said many times by numerous people, "I don't know how to pray or what to pray for." For many Believers who say this, they don't understand the power or magnitude of prayer. Prayer is an everyday tool, and I dare say, it's a necessary tool for the Believer. Prayer is essential to a Believer like breathing is to every living being. Without the ability to breath, we die. Without prayer we die too, not a physical death, but a spiritual death. When we don't pray, we lose our connection to our very lifeline, to our God. There is a saying that goes, "Much prayer, much power, little prayer, little power." Yes, it is that essential!

Unfortunately for many, praying is something to do when we become desperate. In our desperation, after we have tried everything else, then we pray. Most often it's our last resort when in actuality it should be our first response. Prayer allows us to tap into the spirit realm, the heavenly places; it allows us to communicate to God. It allows for our Big Brother, who is Jesus Christ to intercede to the Father on our behalf. "Who is he that condemneth? It is Christ that died, yea rather, that is risen again, who is even at the right hand of God, who also maketh intercession for us," Romans 8:38.

In times of adversity and challenges, many are overwhelmed by what is going on with themselves, their inner circle, and the world as a whole. Our challenges make us look at the problems we are facing. We see the problems but don't see solutions to them. We don't know what to do, and as a result, we become more frustrated, overwhelmed and full of anxiety. As people of habit, our tendency is to ignore the only solution and attempt to resolve the issue within ourselves. Instead of praying, asking God for His wisdom and solution, we do what becomes naturalin our human mindset. And, yes, there are occasions when we do fix it ourselves, or we do find the solution, but on many of these occasions, finding the solution or fixing the problem, we become stressed, overwhelmed, without peace, and sometimes we become ill in the process. When we go to the Lord, in the midst of our trials, tribulation, and problems; when we pray and allow Him to deal with the problem, in return, He gives us His peace that surpasses all understanding. We are able to stand even in the midst of the storm because we have petitioned our prayers to our God. I know what I am talking about because this is what happened to me.

At the age of twenty-three, I was married to a man who was an addict, and as a result of his addiction, I suffered abuse in many forms. God used this relationship, and his addictions to not only get me to run into His arms, but to teach me how to pray. Now I want to say that I was under the illusion like many new believers; that once you give your life to Jesus, everything would be perfect in your life. We heard this from well-meaning Believers who wanted you to receive salvation. I believe they meant well when they were telling us about Jesus, but in their zeal for wanting us to be saved, they gave us a false perception of the Christian walk, an illusion. When the storms in my life kept brewing, I am here to tell you that the illusion died a fast death. I learned very quickly that, yes, the Believer's life is filled with sunny days, but it is also filled with rainy days, and sometimes the rainy days bring tumultuous storms.

During that time in my life, God used everything that was happening to me to push me into my place of prayer. My prayer closet became a place of refuge. God's word, His presence, and prayer became my lifeline. I didn't know what God was doing in my life, or where he was taking me because I was young, on my second marriage, afraid and confused, and I wasn't considered "good" church material. I didn't fit the "good church girl"mold. Simply put, I had been through some stuff, and my life was a mess. Everything that could go wrong went wrong. The night I got born again, God said to me "You should go get what you came here for because you are going to need it," and need it, I did. I felt like I would lose my mind because I was living in a world of control and emotional manipulation. With every incident, I was driven to God in prayer. He used it as a catalyst to push me to the place of praying for others. It didn't matter that in man's sight I didn't have a right to go to God; I went to him in spite of others. I needed Him, and deep inside I knew He would not send me away. I had heard about His uncon- ditional love. I had tried the world's way; it didn't work, so I felt I didn't have another option. I started to pursue God. Four days after I was born again, I went to church and there was a visiting minister who was teaching about the Holy Spirit with the evidence of speaking in tongues. He said if "you believe this is God come and get it." I went and I got it. That night, I was miraculously filled with the Holy Ghost with the evidence of speaking in tongues. My life literally took a turn for the worse in the natural, but God had another plan to use everything that was out of order in my life for His purpose. The battle between the light and darkness became fierce, heated and it escalated. I lived in crisis mode everyday. Prayer became my life source. It was like being in the ocean with nothing but water all around me; I couldn't see land in any direction. All I had was a flotation device. Prayer was my flotation device. I was relentless and pursued God in prayer because my life literally depended on it. He took my crazy life full of darkness to train me for His king- dom. The situation demanded prayer because of my troubled marriage and my husband's drug addiction. He had a cocaine habit that cost a hundred-dollars a day. The world of drug ad- diction is one of endless confusion, fear, fights and threats. I started to pray for His salvation and deliverance and also for his friends. Constantly, I prayed for them, literally everyday. Everything and everyone that passed through my life or was related to me or in relationship with me were on my prayer list. My conversion was so complete that I knew that God could do anything and prayer was the key. This was the path that God used to reveal that my ministry was intercession. Intercession is the sacrificial and selfless act of praying for others. I have a friend who always says that God will get you to do something by function or title. It was ten years before I knew I was an intercessor. Sure people called me a prayer warrior, but I never paid attention. Once I was saved, my reaction to life challenges was prayer. Nevertheless, in February 1996, God sent an evangelist to the church where I was a member. He called me out of my seat and told me my name; he had never seen me before. He said that when God call you by name you have a ministry. He proceeded to tell me that my ministry was intercession. That was when I knew that I was an intercessor; I did it by function, because even now, I believe with all my being that God answers prayer. Through my pain, my calling was birthed. It all started with me praying to my Father.

Through prayer, I learned that I was called to be an Intercessor; this was my assignment. You may not be called to be an Intercessor, but as a Believer you are called to pray. You are called to intercede for others. Through your prayers, the captives are set free, people are healed, and deliverance takes place, peoples lives are transformed, transitioned, and they become whole. Through your prayers and intercession, nations are restored, governments becomes unbound, strongholds and principalities are taken down, and God becomes a Light in the darkness.

For such a time like this, as Believers we need to pray for the un-Believers, our family, our families, countries, nations, and governments. We need to pray like never before. It's our duty. It's a mandate from God.

WHY WE PRAY

Prayer simply put is a conversation with God. It's the primary way that we communicate with God. Prayer was His idea. Yes, God desires for us to talk with him and He with us. In the book of Hebrews, 4:16 it states, "Therefore let us draw near with confidence to the throne of grace, so that we may receive mercy and find grace to help in time of need." God has issued an open invitation to us that we have access to come before Him at any time, day or place. Take God at His word and come to Him in prayer. He is waiting to meet and answer you.

Prayer is a divine assignment because it was initiated by a Divine being, the Prince of Peace, Almighty God, King of Kings and Lord of Lords, the Creator of the heavens and earth. His desire has always been to be engaged in the affairs of men from the beginning of time or the creation of the world. Believe it or not, prayer was God's idea. He has invited you and awaits your RSVP. He wants to have daily regular conversation or fellowship with men since the time of Adam. This activity still holds a place of preeminence with God. Especially for the Believer, the reason for this is that it is our divine assignment. Now even though it was His idea, we, or mankind as a whole reap the benefits of the practice of prayer. It is the place where we can include and inform God of all that is happening in our lives. Prayer gets God involved the affairs of man. He wants us to tell Him of all that concerns us: our woes, sorrows, triumphs and victories. Like a friend or family member, He wants to be in the know, because He possesses the power to change everything. The Bible states in Luke 1:37, "For with God nothing shall be impossible." Yes, my friend through prayer we access God's unlimited power. Even more than our earthly fathers, He loves us and wants nothing but the best for all of us. As we embrace our divine assignment, let us partner with God to bring His will and plan into the earth.

In prayer, there is no distance, and there is no distance with God. When we pray, God is able to move across the world to intervene in the lives of those that we bring to Him through prayer. He is concerned about everything that is important to us. The Bible states in Philippians 4:6, "Be anxious for nothing, but in everything by prayer and supplication with thanksgiving let your request be made known to God." God has not only invited us to pray but has instructed us to pray about everything. Whatever the situation, circumstances or challenge, God wants us to come to Him in prayer.

The Essentials to Effective Prayer

Webster's definition of prayer is an earnest request; the act or practice of addressing a divinity esp. in petition. The Strong's Greek/Hebrew dictionary definition of prayer is a wish expressed as a petition to God. One of our first encounter with prayer is when we pray the sinner's prayer, Romans 10:9-10, "That if thou shalt confess with thy mouth the Lord Jesus, and shalt believe in thine heart that God hath raised him from the dead, thou shalt be saved. For with the heart man believeth unto righteousness; and with the mouth confession is made unto salvation."

After this prayer we are born-again or saved. Immediately we become new creatures, 2 Corinthians 5:17, "Therefore if any man be in Christ, he is a new creature: old things are passed away; behold, all things are become new." Now you are a believer and prayer is vital. This is only the beginning of the transformation of the Believer's life. His desires and focus are to get to know God and establish a relationship. Just to reiterate what I already stated, prayer in the life of a believer is as blood in the human body or a cell phone to a teenager.

Prayer is one of the most beneficial habits a Believer can develop in his/her walk with God. It also creates an intimate relationship with God. When we pray, we are refreshed, repaired, restored, and released. This comes from being in the presence of God-naked, no pretense, no walls… accepted as we are.

In Luke 18:1 Jesus spoke a parable that we are always to pray and not to faint and 1Thessalonians 5:16 states, "Pray without ceasing."

From these two verses we know prayer is not just important but necessary. Now let us look at the essentials of effective prayer. In James 5:16, … "The effectual fervent prayer of a righteous man availeth much." The Amplified Bible says it this way, "The earnest heartfelt continued prayer of a righteous man makes tremendous power available, dynamic in its working." Prayer is a powerful thing.

THE ESSENTIALS TO EFFECTIVE PRAYER ARE:

1. The word of God - Isaiah 55:11; 1Jn. 5:14-15; Jn.15: 7
   - The word and the will of God are one and the same. The word of God clearly tells His will. God will perform His word.
   - Jesus used the word in His temptation/ battle against the enemy. Luke 4:1-13
   - The word is the sword of the Spirit. Ephesians 6:17

2. Knowing your authority – Matthew 18:18
   - Authority in the name of Jesus - Philippians 2: 9-11

3. Praying in the name of Jesus – John 14:13-14; 16:23-24
   - Signs follow His name- Mark 16:17-18
   - Ask in his name – John 15:16

4. Ask in faith – Mark 11:24
   - Faith Believes – Mark 9:23-24
   - Faith is a key to effective praying because without faith we cannot please God. Hebrews 11:6
   - Faith works by love — Galatians 5:6
   - The prayer of faith – James 5:13-16

5. Answered prayer- Matthew 7:7-8

6. Forgiveness – Matthew 6:14-15
   - Forgiveness is necessary because nothing in the Kingdom works unless we forgive. Matthew 18: 21-27, 35; Mark 11:24-25

- Forgiving yourself is also essential. Simply put, if God forgave you, how can you hold it against yourself? Psalms 103:3 Forgave others, you included.

7. Giving thanks-Ephesians 5:20
   - Thanksgiving is also very important and will keep you focus on God's ability not your own. Philippians 4:6-7; Thessalonians 5:18 Psalm 34:1-4
   - Thanksgiving is, at this time, more than any other, a sacrifice. We are encouraged to offer thanks continually. Hebrews 13:15

8. Praying in Tongues –The gift of the Holy Spirit
   - The gift promised - Acts 1:8; 2:1-4
   - Assist us in prayer when we don't know what to pray. - Romans 8:26-27
   - Builds you up. Jude 20
   - You speak mysteries to God. 1Corinthians 14:2

   A. Things to Remember While you wait for your Answer
   - Pray the solution not the problem.
   - The word of God is the solution.
   - Find scripture to stand on, meditate on and confess until you get your answer.
   - What you say in prayer is as important as what you say when you are not praying.
   - Keep a dated prayer list or journal for prayer request.
   - Keep a prayer log for answered prayer. Use this when you need to be reminded that God answers prayer. In times when it seems like nothing is happening read it and be encouraged.

Types of Prayer

We have a unique and exquisite privilege of communicating with God through prayer. Along with this privilege, there is some knowledge that will make our prayers more effective. Even though prayer is God's idea, we benefit from it immensely. One of those benefits is knowing what prayer to pray and what type we should use in any given situation.

The Prayer of Agreement is a prayer that is based on or has its roots in the promise in the Bible in the book of Matthew. Matthew 18:19 states, "Again I say to you, that if two of you agree on earth about anything that they may ask, it shall be done for them by My Father who is in heaven." This prayer promises the Believer that if he and another agree in prayer about something on earth, the Father in heaven will do it for them.

Now before I talk about the next kind of prayer, I would like to say that everything we do in Christ is through faith. Faith is the currency of the kingdom of God. What we do with money in the world is the same thing we do with faith in the kingdom of God. Hebrews 11:6 states, "But without faith it is impossible to please Him, for he who comes to God must believe that He is, and is a rewarder of those who diligently seek Him." Just as money is used to purchase stuff in the earth, faith is used to get what we need from heaven. Whatever we need from God we have to get it by faith, and this pleases Him.

With that being said, the next type of prayer is The Prayer of Faith. The Bible states in James 5:14, "And the prayer of faith shall save the sick and the Lord shall raise him up and if he has committed sins they shall be forgiven him." This is the prayer that we pray when we need to access or reinforce our covenant of salvation in the earth. This is when we exercise our rights and authority as believers. We practice the prayer of faith when we pray for the sick and lead others to salvation in Christ.

Corporate prayer takes place when we as believers are gathered together. Matthew 18:20 states, "For where two or three are gathered together in my name, there am I in the midst of them." There is multiplied power when believers congregate together. Like the prayer of agreement, corporate prayer is the unification of believers in prayer to take possession of what Christ has already purchased for us through his blood. The presence of God, and anointing of the Holy Spirit as we are gathered together, creates an atmosphere that propels us to a place of faith that brings the reassurance that our prayers will be answered.

The Prayer of Consecration and Dedication is often a time of prayer where we set aside time individually or corporately for prayer and fasting. This prayer is usually focused and intense for seeking God for His will, wisdom, and direction for our lives.

The Prayer of Petition or supplication is the prayer where we go before God to ask or petition Him for something specific or to become involved in something that involves us. In Philippians 4:6 the word states, "Be careful for nothing but in everything by prayer and supplication with thanksgiving let your requests be made known unto God. This scripture clearly invites us to ask our heavenly Father for what we need. I would like to say that as Believers we have become very proficient in this and that is great.

Nevertheless, this same scripture verse talks about thanksgiving, so there is a prayer of Thanksgiving. The Prayer of Thanksgiving is the one that is connected to the prayer of petition. It comes into place when you have made your requests to God and as you wait for an answer. In your season of waiting, you exercise your faith as you give thanks to God. This says that I trust that you heard me, and I am confident that you will answer. The Prayer of thanksgiving tells God that you trust Him to keep His promises and that you know He will do what He has promised. Giving thanks in advance is your stamp on the package that insures it will be delivered.

As believers, we are in a war and like those who go to war, we are fighting a battle with the enemy. The Bible states in 2 Corinthians 10:4, "For the weapons of our warfare are not carnal but mighty through God to the pulling down of strongholds." John 10:10 says, "The thief cometh not but to steal, and to kill and to destroy." God has provided a complete suit of armor or warrior gear for battle in Ephesians 6:10-18. This is the reason we have and pray warfare prayers. Warfare prayers are the prayers that we engage in to rout the plans and attacks of the enemy. As we engage in these prayers, we exercise delegated authority as Believers given to us by our Lord and Savior Jesus Christ over the enemy. Our chief commander has provided weapons of war for us to use in battle. One of these weapons is the principal of binding and loosing that is explained in Matthew 18:18, by Jesus. "Verily I say unto you, "Whatever he shall bind on earth shall be bound in heaven: and whatsoever he shall loose on earth is loosed in heaven." There are other weapons like the blood and the name of Jesus; our authority over all the power of the enemy and the sword of the Spirit which is the word of God. God has also provided the armor of God to protect us in battle. Although Jesus has already defeated the enemy, we must enforce His victory in this earth. We need to take our place as the sons of God and remind the enemy that he's defeated.

No book has a list of every prayer; however, the prayers in this book, "Prayers That Touch Heaven and Change Earth" are a great start to begin your prayer journey. I pray that they will help you and assist you as you engage in the benefits of prayer. I pray that as you pray these prayers, God hears you, and change is manifested. I pray that your prayers touch heaven and change earth. Now let us pray!

Ethlyn Ottley Farrell

Prayer for the Government

Father, You said first of all supplication, prayers, intercession and giving of thanks should be made on behalf of all men; first for those in authority, that we may lead a peaceable and godly life with all godliness and honesty.

Therefore, we bring before You the leaders of_____. We lift up the President, the Vice President, the Senate, the House of Representatives, the mayors, the governors, police men and women, and every leader in authority over us in any capacity. We pray that the Spirit of the Lord rest on them, and that Your Spirit of Wisdom gives them the understanding and ability to do what is right and acceptable unto You and the people they have authority over. Lord, we thank You that they have a reverential fear of You and You make them of quick understanding as they walk in the fear of the Lord that they do not judge after what their own ears hear or eyes see, but are led by You and Your Holy Spirit. Lord, give them the courage and the fortitude to make sound decisions that would benefit the common good of the people and not just a selected few. Lord, give them a mouth that confesses You, a boldness to do what is right and a heart that thirst after You and Your righteousness. Let their light shine so all can see that it is You working in them to do what is pleasing, good and acceptable for the people who they have authority over.

We ask You to surround our leaders with men and women of integrity, wisdom and honesty. Give our leaders a readiness to listen to counsel from them, for in the multitude of counselors there is safety. Lord remind our leaders that they were elected as servants of the people and give them the wisdom necessary to serve. Put innovative ideas in their hearts that they may find-ways to balance the budget to benefit all who it concern. Let them put their political parties' differences aside and work together to be a blessing to the people they govern. Help them to cut back government perks, glorified benefits and cut excessive spending, and commit to reinvesting these resources back into the general budget to help the people. Help the leaders to create for the people, a Cost of Living Index that would allow them to give the employees' salaries so that they will be able to live comfortably in our economic climate. Your word says that blessed is the nation whose God is the Lord, so we declare that our_____ are blessed because You are our Lord.

We also lift up the coming elections to You and asking that You would give to us wisdom so that we would elect the right leaders for our nation. Give us knowledge, insight, foresight with wisdom that we are able to elect the person you have ordained to lead this great nation. You said that if we Your people (us) who are called by Your name will humble ourselves and pray and seek Your face and turn from our wicked ways; You will hear from heaven, forgive our sins and heal our land. As we are obedient to Your word, we thank You for Your divine intervention and guidance. Lord, we pray that whoever is elected in office that we, the people will pray for that person(s). As we pray for them, You will hear our prayers, and make all the crooked things straight. Purge our government from greedy, deceitful, unscrupulous person(s) who agenda is contradictory to Yours. Expose the hearts of them that are for You and those who are against You. Allow Your plan to be established in our government.

Father, protect our policemen and women as they serve and protect us. Give them courage to apprehend, pursue and overtake the crime and criminals in our community. Let the citizens who assist them in bringing solutions to cases be protected from any form of retribution or harm. Give our officers wisdom and discretion as they do their jobs as servants of the people. Let them be honest men with integrity and respect. Remove all corruption, hypocrisy and maliciousness from the police force and our government. Father, You said when the righteous is in authority the people rejoice. Lord we thank You for their courage, obedience, self-control, their leadership, service and their heart for You and the people they serve. Lord, we thank You for all You have done, doing and going to do in their lives. As Your Kingdom come on earth as it is heaven, in Jesus name, Amen.

Praying for Our Church Leaders

Father God, we come before with a heart of compassion for the leaders of Your Church bringing them to You in prayer. Lord forgive us for not praying for them as You have asked us to and for indulging in any gossip, conversation, criticism or whatever words that we have spoken that are contrary to Your plan. We come before You with a heart of repentance, asking for Your mercy and a chance to do Your will. We ask You by the power of the Holy Spirit to help us to pray that earnest, heartfelt continued prayer of a righteous man that makes tremendous power available dynamic in its working.

We cover them with Your blood and hedge them in with a hedge of protection and declare that no evil will come by them or their dwelling for they dwell in peaceable habitations, secure dwellings, and quiet resting places. Lord, we declare that no weapon formed against them will prosper and every tongue that raises against them in judgment shall be shown to be in the wrong. We don't use our time to criticize them but we choose to pray for them. We surround them with our faith and love and ask You to help them to stand having done all to stand. Strengthen them for every assignment that You have called them to and keep them focus on You. Surround them with people who will pray for and support them in whatever is Your will and vision for them. Help them to protect, feed and train Your sheep that You have given them the responsibility to lead. Give them an Aaron and Hur as You gave Moses to hold up their hands as they walk through their battles to victory. We pray for the vision that You have entrusted them with to build up your people, that it will edify and strengthen the flock. We pray that the eyes of their understanding be enlightened that they may know what is the hope of their calling in Christ Jesus. Keep them focus on their assignment. Keep them from pride, and keep them humbled as a servant like Jesus was when He came down from Heaven, for He came to be a servant. Allow them to be tenacious and stay on assignment until your Kingdom come and your will is done on earth as it is in heaven in Jesus name, Amen.

Prayers for Marriage: Husband & Wives

Father God, I come boldly before your throne of Grace so we can find grace and mercy to help in time of need.

Father God, help me/us to be quick to forgive, quick to repent and quick to believe. To forgive one another even as God for Christ sake has forgiven me/us.

I decree and declare that _____ __and I walk in love, practice love and speak the truth in Love. First Corinthians 13:4 states: "Love is patient, love is kind. It does not envy, it does not boast, it is not proud. It is not rude, it is not self-seeking, it is not easily angered, and it keeps no record of wrongs. Love does not delight in evil but rejoices with the truth, it always protects always trusts, always hopes, and always perseveres. Love never fails."

I decree and declare that we are doers of your word, not hearers only.

I decree and declare we are swift to hear and slow to speak and slow to wrath.

I decree and declare that every word spoken against my/these marriages, whether by me/us or others DIE NOW in the name of Jesus. Lord set a guard at the door of my mouth and keep watch at the gate of my lips; as my lips speak words of life.

I bind and release every spirit of separation and divorce from their assignments against_____.

I decree and declare that any relationship contrary to God's will for_____and my marriage DIE NOW in the name of Jesus.

I come against the Spirit of adultery, fornication, pornography, lesbianism or homosexuality and any other form of perversion unknown to me but known to God in the name of Jesus. I command them to DIE in the name of Jesus. I bind them and loose them from their assignment around this marriage, in the name of Jesus.

I decree and declare every familiar spirit from generational, inherited or ancestral allegiance, or whatever source must desist their maneuvers against these couples.

I speak forth restoration and deliverance according to Joel 2:25 "And I will restore to you the years that the locust hath eaten, the cankerworm, the caterpillar, and the palmerworm, my great army which I sent among you." I decree and declare wholeness, peace, unity and wisdom for ____ in the name of Jesus.

The husbands will love their wives as Christ loves the church and the wives will submit to the husbands as a service to the Lord.

I decree and declare these unions will stand for what God has put together, let no man put asunder, in the name of Jesus.

I decree and declare my/ these marriages are blessed to be a blessing, in Jesus name. They are established on the word of God, the sword of the Spirit. I cover my marriage with the blood of Jesus and declare them a success in the name of Jesus. We give the word of GOD first place in our homes, lives, and relationships in Jesus name.

Thank You God for open communication and non-bias compromise in_____marriage. Thank You for the power of agreement in prayer as we strive to make prayer a daily priority. _____marriage is a work in progress, and I know that You, Father God is love personified. Thank You for continually showing me how to love_____in the name of Jesus Christ, Amen.

In Romans 8:37, "In all things we are more than conquerors through him that love us. For I am persuaded that neither death, nor life, nor angels, nor principalities, nor powers, nor things present, nor things to come, nor height, nor depth, nor any other creature shall be able to separate us from the love of God, which is in Christ Jesus our Lord. AMEN.

Ethlyn Ottley Farrell

Prayer for Marriage

    Father, in the name of Jesus, I come to You asking You to divinely, intervene into this marriage that You ordained. Help us to surrender to Your will and to forgive one another even as God for Christ has forgiven us. Let Your unconditional love be the catalyst that brings us together in prayer. Teach us to walk in the Spirit so that we will not fulfill the lust of the flesh. Transform us into the couple that You have designed us to be through the power of Your love and the strength of Your grace.

    Remind us of Your word that states that marriage is honorable and the bed undefiled; please show us how to protect our relationship from anything that will bring division and destruction. This covenant of marriage was planned, initiated and instigated by You. Your word states that the husband should leave his father and mother and be joined to his wife and two becomes one flesh. Help to dwell with his wife with knowledge, giving her honor as the weaker vessel, so that their prayers are not hindered. As he submits to You, allow Your love that is in his heart to create an environment that give her the release, of peace and joy, with understanding and pleasure to submit to him in love. Because_____have made a covenant between You and us, _____ have the assurance from your word that a three strand cord is not easily broken. Let our communication be honest and with integrity, like a good meal is seasoned with salt, as we speak the truth in love. May Your love in us be released, as we love each other without fear but with total abandonment. Let our marriage be an sample and ensample, a light in the darkness for others. Gives us wisdom as we grow older, and our bodies are no longer what they used to be. Let us continue to dwell with each, pleasing each other even into our golden years. Let us seek You with our whole heart as we acknowledge You in all our ways, direct our paths in this marriage in the name of Jesus, Amen.

Ethlyn Ottley Farrell

Intimacy in Marriage

Father, Your word states that we are always to pray and not to faint, give up or lose heart. So we come to You asking You to help us to be the couple, partners, and friends that You have designed us to be in this marriage. We do not look only for sexual intimacy but intimacy in every area of this relationship. Let our communication be open as we speak the truth in love with kindness and gentleness with the knowledge that a soft answer turns away wrath. Help us not to love in word only but in deed and truth. May we never use the gift of sexual intimacy as a weapon and do not deprive one another except by agreement for a time of prayer and fasting then come back together so that Satan will not tempt us because of our lack of self-control. Let us be able to recognize and take authority over every strategy of the enemy to bring division, confusion and strife. May my spouse love me as Christ loves the church and give honor to me as the weaker vessel. As a spouse, let me respect my spouse. Remind us by Your Spirit to protect and guard our relationship as we build sustainable avenues of intimacy. May our love be built on Your love and may we walk in it, exemplifying Your love. I thank You for purity in my marriage, heal the wounds of prior relationships, and uproot every familiar spirit from my past including my childhood. Help me to transfer my pain and the shame of those experiences to You. Eradicate all ungodly thoughts that seek to influence my actions and behaviors. I declare freedom to fully give myself to my spouse, never defrauding him/her and creating an environment that invites all that's good to manifest in the sanctity of our bed. Lord I continue to trust You to cause the intimacy physically, emotionally and mentally to develop in this marriage in the name of Jesus, Amen.

SURVIVING DIVORCE

Father, I come to You in my brokenness with a broken-heart, which I know only You can heal. I know that You hate divorce, and now I understand why because of the destructive results of it, but I know that You love me. You have made me a survivor of this tragedy, for You have a special purpose for me. Lord, you promised not to leave me nor forsake me and I believe Your word. I ask You to remove the pain, shame, scorn, hate and anger that I have projected on myself and that I feel from others. I choose to forgive those who have hurt me and release them, as I forgive myself also. Let Your love overshadowed all that is within me that's not of You. Lord, You are the Lord God that heals, so heal me, Father, for men look at the outward appearance, but You look at the heart. I am asking You to heal my mind, will and emotions, as You restore my soul as only You can. Divinely remove every tormenting thought that plague my mind and help me to bring every thought into the captivity to the obedience of Jesus Christ. Allow me to focus and keep my eyes on You, the Author and Finisher of my faith, as I renew my mind in Your word. I desire that You distribute Your healing power to every hidden area of my heart as You create in me a clean heart and renew a right spirit within me. I ask You to bring life from death as only You can do; for what is impossible with men, is possible with You. Allow me to experience Your unconditional love as You touch me with Your grace in every aspect of my life, as You heal all my wounds and restore me to health. Fill me up with renewed hope through Jesus Christ who is the hope of glory. Open my heart so that I can embrace the future and the new beginning that You have created for me as I walk in newness of life. Everything the enemy meant for bad turn it around for good. Father I trust You with my life. Let Your plan and will be established in my life once again by Your resurrection power and everlasting love, in the name of Jesus, Amen.

Prayer for Children

We come in the name of Jesus, speaking and praying Your word, as we stand in the gap, praying for our children that are blessings from You, Lord, the fruit of the womb which is Your reward; who have been called for such a time as this.

I decree and declare that they walk worthy of the Lord fully pleasing Him and desiring to please Him in all things.

I decree and declare that they have a hunger and thirst for righteousness and are being filled.

I come against every spirit of distraction and worldly influence that rise up as a nuisance in their path in the name of Jesus, and I curse them from the root and loose them from their assignment against these children/young people. Let them stand up for the truth and refuse to compromise in what they believe. Your word is truth, and You watch over Your word to perform it. I decree and declare that the eyes of their understanding are enlightened and they know the hope of their calling.

I decree and declare that they walk in your wisdom and that they listen to counsel and are wise. I declare that they are obedient, listen, respect and adhere to authority. I declare that the ones that have authority over them by relationship, school or community, that You will give them the ability with wisdom to keep guard over them and protect them, from any hurt, harm or danger. We come against any wicked, pedophile, vile or corrupt spirit that would try to infiltrate their presence or come into contact with our children. We plead the blood of Jesus over our children, and thank You that You are always watching over them, even when we are not able to. We thank You that they will do well in school and in all of their endeavors. We thank You that they will grow up to be good standing people in their community, and in their nation. They are a light in the darkness. We thank You that they will be effective tools and set the example for other children and as a result, a generation will come to know Jesus because of their light.

They have ears to hear and hearts to receive what the Spirit of the Lord says.

Thank You that their influence comes from You and their heart is after You. As they have been trained up in the way they should go and when they are old they will not depart from it.

We decree and declare that every trap, snare and ambush set for them comes to naught. I decree and declare that they recognized the traps of the enemy and go far from them.

We declare their hearts are after You and they are open to Your guidance. We decree and declare that Your Spirit leads them.

Father, I pray that these children/young people are full of peace; all turmoil, strife and confusion are bound and loose from them. Father, I thank You that they know their purpose and seek You for wisdom. Give them strength to stand having done all to stand. Bless them in all their endeavors as You lead and direct them to their callings, careers and professions that You have ordained for them. Let Your Kingdom come and Your will be done in their lives on earth as it is in heaven, in the name of Jesus.

Now Lord, give them favor with men as they have with You, surround them with favor as with a shield. You are Jehovah Jireh, our provider, who provides the finances that are needed for their education and every other need that they have, monetary or otherwise.

Remind them by Your Holy Spirit, that You are their source and a cattle on a thousand hills are Yours and it's Your good pleasure to give your children the kingdom.

Father, I thank You for your blessings that make rich and

add no sorrow to it. Let Your plan and will be established in their lives. Now Father those who don't know you draw them by Your Spirit and allow them to come into a relationship with You through Your Son, the Lord Jesus Christ. Teach them their value and help them to guard their sexuality until marriage.

I decree and declare that every trap and plan of the enemy for their life is untraceable in the realm of the spirit and completely destroyed. I command spirits of fornication, adultery, generational and ancestral familiar spirits to be bound and loose from their assignment against them. As these spirits try to track them, they cannot be traced or found because Your blood is around them. Any relationship that's not of You, we curse it and declare it broken in the name of Jesus.

Father, thank You for ordering their footsteps and showing them they way to go. Direct, guide and lead them in a plain path for Your namesake, in Jesus name, Amen.

Ethlyn Ottley Farrell

Prayer for Our School Systems

Father, we bring our school systems to You because You said that You will perfect that which concerns us. Our desire is for them to come into alignment with Your word and promises as Your kingdom come on earth as it is in heaven. You have said that whatsoever we desire when we pray believe that we receive it and we will have it. We believe Your word and You watch over Your Word to perform it. Now we ask You to direct the hearts of those who are in positions of authority that makes decisions concerning our school systems. Influence their policies by Your word and, surround them with wise counsel, for in the multitude of counselors there is safety. Let them come before You to ask for wisdom and direction as they make informed decisions to guide our children and impact our schools. Divinely interfere in any legislation that is contradictory to Your plan. Allow educators that are believers, to be hired so they can pray covertly to dispel all perversion that is targeted for this system. Place them in jobs and positions of influence so they have leverage to transform the schools. Raise up a generation that will cause prayer to be reinstated in our schools. Give them boldness and wisdom to work within the system rules; surround them with favor as with a shield, give them favor with men as they have with You. Send them with Your power, love and grace to be a force to be reckoned with for good. Let them work in synchronized unity one with another so Your plans will be established and bring forth change for the best. May the moral temperature in our school system begin to reflect Your glory as we call those things that be not as though they are. Thank You Lord for all You have done, what You are doing and everything You are going to do, in Jesus name, Amen.

Prayer for Families Going Through Separation and Divorce

Father, I bring _____family/families before You and we know divorce is not Your best but, You are a God of mercy. I ask You to comfort _____ who are facing this challenge. Hide _____ under Your shadow of the Almighty God. Give _____ wisdom in every area of _____ lives so that _____ makes good decisions, not ones that are emotionally driven, as faith triumph over feelings. Help _____ to trust in the Lord Jehovah, for in the Lord Jehovah is everlasting strength. Let You be _____ first choice to run to, as You remind _____ that the name of the Lord is a strong tower, and the righteous run into it and they are safe.

_____ takes authority over the spirit of rejection, condemnation, despair, hopelessness and depression. _____ come against un-forgiveness, anger, hatred and bitterness. _____ bind every spirit of darkness that has been dispatched against them and breakdown every stronghold of the enemy in the name of Jesus. _____ command you to back off NOW! You have got to go; for God has given _____ authority to tread on serpents and scorpions and over all the power of the enemy and nothing by any means shall harm_____.

_____ also prays for the children in these family/families. Father help them to know that they are not at fault nor to blame for this situation. Deliver _____ from rebellion, peer pressure, anger, lashing out, violence, guilt, shame, depression, thoughts of suicide and rejection. Lord, please do not let _____ be lured into a gang at this season of great vulnerability because of _____ need to belong. Protect _____ from the enemy deceptive traps, every attack of emotional turmoil and distress.

Lord help _____ not to feel like they have to choose one parent over the other, nor that they are caught in the middle of this confusion and conflict. Let _____ be sensitive to the parent who has stayed with them and has been left behind; knowing that they are also hurting. Protect _____ in the midst of this place of pain, shame, abandonment and death. Remind _____ that even when _____ walk through the valley of the shadow of death that You are with_____. Father release Your mercy as You heal every thought and symptom of distress, in the name of Jesus.

Lord, heal the broken hearts and lives of this family/families. Give them Your grace to carry on; overtake them with Your love. Comfort them in this place and let them experience hope through Jesus Christ who is the hope of glory. Father give them supernatural strength and the divine ability to keep their eyes on You the author and finisher of their faith no matter what the reality looks like. Reassure_____ that You are working this out for good, in the name of Jesus, Amen.

Prayer for Forgiving Yourself and Others

Lord, You said that I must come to your throne of Grace boldly so that I can find grace and mercy to help in time of need. I want Your help for I need to forgive _____, just like You have forgiven me. I am hurting and don't feel like for- giving_____, but I walk by faith and not by sight. Therefore, I choose to be obedient to Your word and forgive just as God for Christ sake forgave me. You told Peter that if a brother sins against him, he should forgive him every time, and he did it. I choose to be a doer of Your word, and I release it and let it go. I chose not to let un-forgiveness have any place or hold on me or in my life. I chose not to be offended. I chose to allow Your grace to minister to me in this place of un-forgiveness. I chose to love in spite of how I feel. I thank You that the Holy Spirit is strengthening me in my inner man in this area. I forgive_____now in the Name of our Lord, Jesus Christ. AMEN.

Ethlyn Ottley Farrell

Prayer for Rededication for Backslidden Believers

Father of mercy and grace, I come before You humbly asking for Your forgiveness. Like the prodigal son, I have strayed away from Your ways and did my own thing, and as a result of doing it my way and following my course, I ended up in a mess of my own making. But now I have come to my senses and desire to return to You, my first Love. I am asking You to forgive me of my sins and wash me afresh in the blood of my Savior, the Lord Jesus. Refresh me with the gentleness of Your love and Your sweet, precious Holy Spirit. Make me new and restore to me the joy of my salvation. Fan up the flame once again, and rekindle the fire that once burned so brightly. Order and direct my steps once again. Place a hunger and thirst for righteousness within me and help me to seek Your kingdom first and all things will be added unto me.

Thank You Father God for all you have done and all that you are going to do. In Jesus Name. AMEN

Prayer of Thanksgiving

Father God, I come to You with thanksgiving and praise from a grateful heart.

I am acknowledging Your goodness and faithfulness to me giving You the honor and glory that is due to Your name.

I am extending to You adoration and glory because You are worthy of all praise. I exalt You, Lord.

Thank You for Your goodness and Your mercies, for Your mercies endures forever. Your mercies are new every morning. Great is thy faithfulness! Your loving kindness is everlasting and true.

Thank You for handling all my cares, worries, anxieties, problems and concerns.

Thank You for blessing me with a new life and a new beginning every day.

Thank You for perfecting all that concerns me, and making all the crooked places straight in my life.

Thank You for forgiving all my iniquities and healing all my diseases. Thank You for healing, delivering and saving my family and friends.

Thank You for my salvation and Your joy, which is my strength, for in Your presence, there is fullness of Joy. You are faithful, and I am grateful.

Thank You for Your peace that surpasses all understanding. Thank You for Your loving kindness, Your gentleness, Your long-suffering and for caring for me. Thank you for forgiving me, in spite of my failings, my disobediences and my flaws. Thank You for Your Word, for Your Word is a lamp unto my feet. Your Word is a light in darkness.

Thank You for Your blessings that maketh rich, and You add

no sorrow to it. Thank You for divine health, a good life, and for healing me of all my iniquities and sickness.

Thank You for being the awesome, magnificent and wonderful Father that you are.

Father God, I offer You the sacrifice of praise, the fruit of my lips giving, thanks to Your name continually, in Jesus Name, AMEN.

Prayer for Direction

Father, You said in your word that the steps of a righteous man are ordered of the Lord. As _____ come before You asking You for direction, make _____ pathway brighter and brighter until the full light of day; order _____ footsteps and show _____ the way to go. Lord make a plain path for _____ feet for You promised that You will perfect that which concerns _____. I take authority over any distraction, confusion or illusions that the enemy may try to put in _____ path to delay or throw _____ off the path or direction You have ordained for_____ in the name of Jesus. Lord, _____ wait on You and do not make a move without You. I know that You have plans for _____ for good and not evil to give _____ a hope and a future, an expected end. Lord, _____ trust You with all _____heart and lean not to _____ own understanding, _____ acknowledge You in all (my/her/his) ways, You will direct _____ path in which way to go. Thank You for clear, insightful directions, Father, in Jesus name, Amen.

Ethlyn Ottley Farrell

Praying for Wisdom

 My God and Father, I come to you asking You for wisdom in _____area of _____ life. You said if _____ lack wisdom ask of You and You will give it liberally and upbraideth not. For You stated in Your word that wisdom is the principle thing so get wisdom and with all of our getting get understanding. As _____ receive wisdom from you give _____ insight, foresight, and discernment. _____ take authority over any lies, thoughts or reasoning of the enemy that comes against the knowledge of God and bring every thought into the obedience of Christ. Thank You for the wisdom that is from above that is first pure, then peaceable, gentle and easy to be entreated, full of mercy and good fruits, without partiality and without hypocrisy. I declare that _____ hear Your voice, know Your voice and the voice of a stranger _____ do not follow. Father, it is appreciated that whenever _____ needs wisdom, You have provided an unlimited supply. Thank You for Your wisdom in the name of Jesus, Amen

Renewing the Mind

Father God, I come before You speaking Your word boldly over my mind. I acknowledge every good thing in me is that which is in Christ Jesus. I decree and declare I have the mind of Christ; I hold the thoughts, feelings and purposes of His heart. I decree and declare that I am not conformed to this world, but transformed, by the renewing of my mind, that I may prove what is the good, acceptable and perfect will of God. I am committed to read, study and confess the word over my life as I am a doer of the word and not a hearer only.

Father God, Your will and word is one in the same. Thank you, Lord, my faith works because I walk in love, practice love, and speak the truth in Love.

I think on those things that are good, true, noble, right, pure, admirable, and lovely. If anything is excellent or praise worthy, I think on these things. I keep my mind on You, Father God, and I am in perfect peace. I believe the best of every person. When the enemy comes like a flood, the Spirit of the Lord lifts up a standard against him. I cover my mind with the Blood of Jesus and filter my thoughts through His word. Thank You for a sound mind in Jesus name, Amen.

Ethlyn Ottley Farrell

SALVATION

Lord, salvation is found in no one else but You, for there is no other name under heaven given to mankind by which we must be saved. For You said in Your word, "For it is with your heart that you believe and are justified, and it is with your mouth that you profess your faith and are saved." Truly my soul finds rest in You, Lord, and our salvation comes from You. Father, I thank You that everyone who calls on the name of the Lord will be saved. Father, I thank You that when we accept Jesus as our Lord and Savior, we are no longer Your enemies, but we are now Your sons; we are reconciled to You through the death of Your Son, how much more, having been reconciled, shall we be saved through His life! Lord Jesus, I believe You are the Son of God and that You died and rose from the dead for my sins. Come into my heart and be Lord of my life. For I am not ashamed of the gospel, because it is the power of God that brings salvation to everyone who believes: first to the Jew, then to the Gentile. Thank You for transforming my life now in Jesus name, Amen.

Salvation for the Lost

Father God, You said, "If we ask of You, You will give us the heathen for our inheritance and the utmost ends of the earth for our possession." You said, "If we lift you up from the earth, you will draw all men unto You," so I bring to you the lost and their need for salvation. Lord, You love the world so much, You gave Your only begotten Son so whosoever believes in Him will not perish but have everlasting life. You did not come into the world to condemn the world, but the world through You might be saved.

Draw them to You by Your Spirit for Your word says they can only come to You if the Spirit that You sent draws them.

I take authority over the spirit of blindness that's blinding the eyes of their mind. I bind him and loose him from his assignment against them in the name of Jesus. Lord of the harvest, send forth the perfect laborers in their paths, and give them ears to hear and hearts to receive what Your Spirit is saying. As they respond to the Holy Spirit and Your love draws them to repentance give them a hunger and thirst for righteousness with a strong desire to study Your word. Give them hearts of flesh instead of hearts of stone.

Change their desires from worldly to desires for You and Your Kingdom. Let them seek Your Kingdom first and Your righteousness and everything else will be added to them.

Thank You for this Harvest of Souls, in the name of the Lord Jesus Christ, Amen.

Ethlyn Ottley Farrell

Gathering the End Time Harvest

Lord, we come before Your throne lifting up the end-time harvest knowing that You desire that no one should perish but all come to repentance. Father, give us Your people a strategic plan to minister life to those in this harvest. It is Your love and goodness that draw men to repentance, so we entreat You to draw them to your side by the Holy Spirit because no one comes to You unless the Spirit who You sent draws them. Lord, equip us with Your unending mercy, everlasting love and loving kindness to meet them where they are. As we do this, help us to remind them that You did not come into the world to condemn the world, but that the world through You might be saved. We ask You as Lord of the Harvest, to fill the harvest with laborers as well as make us the laborers in the harvest. Make our words to them like words fitly spoken as apples of silver in settings of gold; help us to speak the truth in love. Turn their hearts to You, melt away every form of resistance with Your goodness and gather them into Your Kingdom as it is established on earth as it is in heaven, in the name of Jesus, Amen.

GREATER WORKS

Father, we come to You in response to the words that our Lord and Savior Jesus Christ declared, "Truly, truly, I say to you, he who believes in Me, the works that I do, he will do also; and greater works will he do because I go to the Father." We desire to do these greater works and be vessels used to manifest them in this age for Your glory. Lord, anoint us afresh with the fire and power of Your Holy Spirit. We plead the blood of Jesus over ourselves and clothe ourselves with the armour of God. We know that without You we can do nothing: but all things are possible with You. So, having done all to stand, we stand having girded our lions with truth and having put on the breastplate of righteousness and having our feet shod with the preparation of the gospel of peace in addition to all, taking the shield of faith to extinguish all the flaming arrows of the evil one, taking the helmet of salvation and the sword of the Spirit, which is the word of God; For it's not by might or power but by Your Spirit everything is done. Let Your love draw men to repentance as we go forth to do our Father's business. Give us wisdom and discernment to flow in the power of the Holy Spirit. Your word declares that as many as are led by the Spirit of God are the sons of God. As Your sons, we thank You that we hear Your voice, know Your voice and the voice of a stranger we do not follow. Lord, we believe Your Word, that You gave us the power to become the sons of God. We walk in that power by faith knowing that in Christ victory is sure in every area of our lives. We take authority over any tactic, strategy, distraction or schemes of the enemy and command them to die now in the name of Jesus. We take our rightful place as the sons of God and walk in newness of life, as we walk in the Spirit and do not fulfill the lust of the flesh. Our eyes are on Jesus, who is the author and finisher of our faith. As we step forward into this new, fresh anointing we go forth with boldness and power, knowing greater is he that is in us than he who is in the world and we are more than conquerors. We declare that we will do greater works as we walk into Your plan for us, in the name of Jesus Christ our Lord, Amen.

HAVING LOVE ONE FOR ANOTHER

Lord, Your word declares that we should love our neighbors as we love ourselves and as a doer of Your word I am obedient to do as You have said. Your love is shed abroad in my heart by Your Holy Spirit that is given unto me, so I am empowered to walk in love, practice and speak the truth in love. It also releases Your ability within me to extend this love to my brothers and sisters in Christ. You said that if I do not love my brother that I see, how can I say I love God whom I have not seen. Lord, I do not love in word only but in deed and truth. This love causes me to forgive even as God for Christ sake has forgiven me. Lord, Your love propels me to a place of peace where there is no fear because perfect love cast out all fear. I know that I have passed from death to life because I love the brethren and love covers a multitude of sins. Father, You love me unconditionally, and I desire to be a child that imitates my Father. I release every hurt, pain, and conflict that has separated me from my brothers and sisters in the faith. I throw off every weight and sin that so easily beset me and run the race that is set before me, looking unto Jesus, the author and finisher of my faith. I can do all things through Christ who strengthen me. Now it is He that works in me to will and do of His good pleasure; who has made me able to walk in love and be a blessing to others in Jesus name, Amen.

Ministry

Father, I come to You in the mighty name of Jesus. Father God, You have called these people and ministries for such a time as this. For this time of divine appointment, go before them open the doors that no man can shut, order their footsteps and show them the way to go. Let Your anointing that's on and in them be a double portion. Allow them to hear Your voice clearly and the voice of a stranger they will not follow.

I take authority over every plan of the enemy to bring confusion and doubt to their minds. I command it to cease. I bind the works of the enemy against their minds, life, family, and ministry. I loose you from your assignment. For this reason, the Son of God was manifested that He might destroy the works of the devil.

I come against every attack of doubt, unbelief, second guessing oneself and anything that will throw them off track or make them turn back. I command you devil to back off of them and stop it in the name of the Lord Jesus Christ. No weapon formed against them will prosper, and every tongue that rises up against them to discourage or speak negative words against the call for their life, family, or ministry will be shown to be in the wrong and condemned.

I decree and declare that there's no fear here, because You, Lord did not give us a Spirit of fear, but of Power, Love and a Sound Mind.

I decree and declare that they walk in boldness and confidence for the righteous is as bold as a Lion.

I decree and declare they humble themselves under the mighty hand of God, and He exalts them in due time.

I pray that the Spirit of the Lord rests upon them. Your Spirit of Wisdom and Understanding, Counsel and Might, and the fear of the Lord. They do not judge after what their own ears hear, and eyes see, but with righteousness, they judge and with equity they reprove and make decisions.

I decree and declare that they walk circumspectly, redeeming the time because the days are evil. They are transparent, honest men and women of integrity, excellence, and accountable to you and the people you have surrounded them with.

I thank You Father God, for surrounding them with people after Your own heart. Those who desire to serve You and Your Kingdom, who are assigned to pray and intercede for them.

I decree and declare that they recognize the Holy Spirit leading and direction in the name of Jesus.

I decree that the Gifts of the Spirit flow through them and that they are a blessing to the Body of Christ.

I decree and declare that_____walk in love, practice love and speak the truth in love because the Holy Ghost, who is given to them, sheds the Love of God abroad in their hearts.

I decree and declare that_____ walk in the Spirit and they will not fulfill the lust of the flesh. That they are quick to hear, slow to speak and slow to wrath and they are walking in the fruits of the Spirit.

Father, God, as You have called us out, we know that You promised to supply all of our needs according to Your riches in Glory in Christ Jesus. Jehovah Jireh is our provider and I thank You that You came to give us life and life more abundantly. Let the resources, finances, and people come in to bring to full fruition all that you have called us to do.

I dispatch the ministering spirits to go forth and bring in everything necessary to bring this work to completion and full manifestation.

I take authority and bind the Spirit of stress, uncertainty, distress, lack, poverty, depression, oppression, rejection, condemnation and un-forgiveness, and loose and render then powerless in the Name of Jesus.

Loose the finances and the men and women of God and let them go in the Name of the Lord Jesus Christ.

Now Father God, thank You for Your plan and provisions and purpose. Let Your Kingdom come and Your will be done.

Thank You that we prosper and are in health even as our souls prospers.

I pray that they remember not the former things, nor consider the things of old, behold I will do a new thing, now it will Spring forth, I will make rivers in the desert and a way in the wilderness.

We cover_____with the Blood of Jesus, spirit, soul, and body, and seal this prayer in the Name of Jesus. AMEN

The Five-Fold Ministry

Father, You said in Your word men are always to pray and not to faint, so we lift up those who are called to the five-fold ministry. Lord, blessed them for being courageous in responding to the call that You have placed on their lives, and for leaving their chosen profession to surrender to Your plan for their lives. Help those who are still struggling to make a decision to walk into Your call and plan for their lives. Activate and release a new level of trust within them as they make the transition from their chosen profession to Your call on their lives. As they seek You, assure them that You will perfect that which concerns them. Remind them to cast all their cares on You because You care for them watchfully and affectionately.

As they trust in You with all their hearts and lean not on their own understanding but in all their ways acknowledge You, You will direct their paths. Lord, You have made provisions for them in all things; as they walk forth to do your will, You will cause a harvest to come into their hands; some thirty, sixty and a hundred fold return.

As they confidently trust in the Lord Jehovah for in Him is everlasting strength. I take authority over fear anxiety and worry; I command it to go in the name of Jesus. Remind them by your Spirit, that You have given them vision, and You will make provision for the vision, for You are Jehovah Jireh, their provider. Lord, encourage and enable them to run to the rock of their salvation as they keep watch for our souls. Father God, protect them from burnout, wrong priorities, man's agenda and the deceit of the enemy. Surround them with a hedge of protection and people who would support them, pray for them and tell them the truth as they hold up their hands in labor, challenges, and battles, like Hur and Aaron did for Moses in war, until victory is attained. Help them to walk-in integrity, accountability and peace; circumspectly redeeming the time for the days are evil. Let us look beyond their faults, see their needs and pray for their divine abilities.

God, You know all things and there is no searching of Your understanding, Your understanding is infinite. As they depend on You, keep their eyes on You, seeking You with their whole hearts, knowing that all things work together for good to those who are called according to Your purpose. As these men and women of God go forth in faithfulness to plant Your word in the hearts of Your people. Shield them from the strategy and attacks of the enemy. I bind every fiery dart and loose them from their assignment against them. I decree and declare that they walk in victory in every area. Thanks be to God, who gives us the victory through our Lord Jesus Christ. Thank You for the harvest that comes forth in them and the lives of others, as they walk in the power of the call that's on their lives, we give You all the glory honor and praise in Jesus name, Amen.

Provision for the Vision

Father, You are a God that is more than enough, You are Jehovah Jireh, our provider. I trust You and believe Your word. You said in Your word, that I should write the vision down, that they that read it may run with it, for the Vision is for an appointed time and though it tarries wait for it for it will surely come to pass. Lord, as I have been obedient to Your word and have done what You said; I have laid out this vision before Your people. With that understanding, I bring this vision that You have impregnated me with before You and lay it at Your feet. I release all the cares, anxiety and worries that plague my soul related to this vision. I cast all my cares upon You for You care for me. Now I stand in agreement with Your people; we refuse to be anxious about anything, but in everything by prayer and supplication, with thanksgiving we let our requests be known to You and the peace of God that passes all understanding keeps our hearts and minds through Christ Jesus. Lord, I know that what is impossible with me is possible with You and all things are possible to them that believe. We ask You to cause our hearts to align with Your plan. Let every provision that is needed to bring this vision to pass be provided naturally and supernaturally. We thank You that we have favor with men as we have with You. Give us innovative and strategic ideas as You cause the cash flow for this vision to multiply. Lord, you came to give us life and life more abundantly. As we trust You and Your provision may every financial need be met in abundance. Allow everything and everyone assigned to this plan to come into place of unity, as we move forward in Your timing, for there is a time and season for everything under the sun. Give us wisdom to execute and authenticate that which You have deposited in our hearts and minds. This is the confidence that we have in You if we ask anything according to Your will You hear us and if we know that You hear us we know we have the petitions that we desire of You. As this vision is fulfilled may the community be blessed and impacted by Your love and mercy. May it be a place of refuge and peace for those in need, filled with Your Spirit, power and peace, as You equip us to be a blessing as we show forth Your glory and grace in Jesus name, Amen.

Business

Father God, You are God. You are my source, my Jehovah Jireh, the one who provides everything for me. You supply my needs according to Your riches in Glory. You said in Your word that if I acknowledge You in all my ways, that You will direct my path. I acknowledge You in my business. Show me the direction and path You want me to go. Holy Father, there's no searching of Your understanding; You know all things. Open my eyes to see the opportunities that are before me. Give me wisdom in all the areas in this business so that I can conduct this business in honor and integrity. Allow me to have favor with men as I have with You. Lord, You said I would stand before kings not mean men. Let your blessings come upon _____ and overtake it. Bless the workstation of my hands like You've promised in Your word.

Send me skilled men and women as You did for Solomon as he built Your temple. Let them be skilled in their craft, profession, and faithful to You, honest that they may be a blessing to _____ and this business a blessing to them. Give me innovative ideas to keep _____ fresh at the top of its game with cutting edge technology and updated data. Release all the creative abilities that You have placed within us to flow, as the original, creative, user-friendly ideas, that is within us come forth to bless and satisfy our customers. Thank You for sending us faithful paying customers, who tell others about this establishment while recommending us to their family and friends. Lord, thank You for imparting to us these phenomenal gifts, supernatural abilities and divine assignments as we get into alignment for Your agenda in this business, as we receive Your best with thanksgiving.

Thank You for being a God that is more than enough and for blessing _____ so that they can be a blessing to people, our community, and Your Kingdom.

As _____ has given into Your Kingdom, cause men to give into this business.

Thank You for marketing strategies and progressive ideas to promote our products and services. Thank You for You have given us all things that pertain to life and godliness.

I decree and declare _____ a success and successful in the Name of the Lord, Jesus Christ. AMEN.

FINANCES

Father God, Thank You that You are Jehovah Jireh, my Provider, and You supply all my needs according to Your riches in glory. There is no limit to Your resources. The cattle on a thousand hills are Yours, and _____ am a joint heir with Jesus; therefore, they are mine as well. I decree and declare that there is no lack in You, so _____ don't lack or want for anything.

Thank You for blessing the work of my hands and causing your blessings to come upon me and overtake me.

Because _____ give, it is given to_____ good measure, pressed down, and shaken together; You will cause men to give into my bosom. Lord, it is You who gives _____ the power to get wealth and cause me to prosper and be in good health even as my soul prospers.

Father, give _____ wisdom in and how to handle wealth and finance, make me a good steward over my talents, wealth, finances, relationships and resources.

As an imitator of You, Father God _____ call those things that be not as though they are, because the blessing of the Lord maketh rich and he adds no sorrow to it. You have given _____ everything that pertains to life and godliness. I have more than enough to take care of myself and be a blessing to others. I have more than enough to put into Your storehouse so others will benefit from the overflow. Thank you in Jesus Name. AMEN.

Ethlyn Ottley Farrell

Knowing God as Our Source

Father God, You are a good Father to and have promised that You will supply all of our needs according to Your riches in glory by Christ Jesus. You cannot lie; so help us to trust Your promises for every provision. Deliver us from the spirit of entitlement, ungratefulness, and ingratitude. Deposit within us a thankful heart as we give praise to Your name, for You Lord, are the source of everything that we need and could desire. We take authority over the spirit of fear and come against every form or disguise in which it presents itself, in the name of Jesus. For You have not given us a spirit of fear but a Spirit of love, power and a sound mind; we submit to God, resist the devil, and he flees from us. You are our very source of life, peace, finances and all that we need and desire. Reassure us that You have engraved us on the palm of Your hand and therefore, nothing can touch us unless it passes through Your hand. Lord, You cause all things to work together for our good because we love You and are call according to Your purpose. You have given us all things that pertain to life and godliness. We give praise and thanks for Your goodness, provision and grace, in Jesus name, Amen.

Understanding the Grace of God

Lord, Your grace is so amazing. I pray that You will help me to understand, accept, and implement it in my life. You were the one who allowed Your grace to find me and save me through faith. It was You who deposited the desire in me to understand Your unmerited favor, which I did not deserve but You generously and lavishly give it to me along with Your unconditional love. Father, Your grace is what continues to change my life, because it is You who work in me to will and do of Your good pleasure. Your Spirit ignites the fire within me to access Your throne of grace that I may obtain mercy and find grace to help in time of need. Father, I pray, that my God, the Father of my Lord Jesus Christ, the Father of glory, will give to me His Spirit of wisdom and revelation in the knowledge of him, that the eyes of my understanding being enlightened, that I may know what is the hope of Your calling and what is the riches of Your glory of the inheritance of the saints and what is the exceeding greatness of His power towards us who believe according to the working of His mighty power, which You wrought in Christ when You raised Him from the dead and set Him at Your right hand in heavenly places, far above all principality and power, might and dominion and every name that's name, not only in this world but also in that which is to come: and has put all things under His feet and gave Him to be head over all things to the church which is His body the fullness of Him that fills all in all. As You impart insight and understanding of Your grace to me, I ask You to help to walk in Your word and plan for my life, because Your word is a lamp to my feet and a light to my path. Thank You that You cause all grace to abound towards me that

Ethlyn Ottley Farrell

I having all sufficiency in all things abound to every good work. Thank You for your grace continuously working on my behalf in Jesus name, Amen.

Singles Looking for a Mate

Father God, in Your word You said to be anxious for nothing but by prayer and supplication with thanksgiving let my request be known to God (You). So I come asking You for a mate. Lord, every good and perfect gift comes down from above, from You. I know that You have a mate for me. I do not want to pick or choose them because of how they look or make me feel, but Father, I desire that You cause us to meet or encounter one another. Father, I want what You want for me; an original person designed for me by You; one who loves me as Christ loves the church, who seek Your Kingdom first and Your righteousness and everything else is added to him/her. I desire my mate's heart to hunger and thirst after Your righteousness, and You will fill them. Put within this person a heart to give and as Your word says it will be given unto him/her good measure, pressed down, shaken together and running over You will cause men to give unto to his/her bosom. Download within_____a spirit of generosity and a heart to establish Your kingdom in this world. I bind all counterfeits, fakes, and impostors, and loose them from their assignments against me. Reveal every person that approaches me that isn't the person for me because everything is open to the eyes of Him with whom we have to do. Lord, I trust You in selecting the mate for me, for I know that you see all things, including the future, so I know if You choose my mate, we can weather the storms of life together. Father, when I look at a person, I tend to see the exterior, but You see the interior, the heart of a person. You see all that I am not able to see, so You will keep me from being deceived, fooled or played.

I thank You that when my mate comes, there will be a peace and witness in my spirit, and You will confirm him/her also.

Lord, keep me pure and chaste even if I'm not a virgin; please control my sexual appetite and give me supernatural help to crucify my flesh and to abstain from sexual immorality. Destroy, erase, and make untraceable all the habits, partnerships, and connections that I acquired through my sexual history. Turn all my desires, physical, mental, emotional, and spiritual, toward you and your kingdom. Eradicate every soul tie, demonic influence, alliance or attachments from the past or current relationship; annihilate them from my future. Cut every umbilical cord from wicked associates and unfriendly friends with evil intentions that are meant for my destruction and demise. I bind every evil spirit of deception and loose it from its assignment against me in the name of Jesus Christ.

I decree and declare that I have clear insight and accurate perception about what the will of the Lord is for my life. You said to remind You of Your word. Your word says it's better to marry than to burn, so I give my desire to marry to You and by doing this, I wait patiently, wholly and quietly on you until my mate is manifested in the natural. Let Your will be done in this area of my life. Every plan that You have for me may it be fulfilled in the correct time and season in the name of Jesus Christ, Amen.

SINGLE AND SATISFIED

Father God, I come before You as a single person committed to You and Your way, asking You to keep me in every area of my life. Lord help to walk in the Spirit, so I will not fulfill the lust of the flesh. I desire to walk worthy of You fully pleasing You in all things; Strengthen me with Your might according to Your glorious power; with all patience and long-suffering with joyfulness. Giving thanks to You who has made me a partaker of the inheritance of the saints in light, who has delivered me from the kingdom of darkness and translated me into the kingdom of Your beloved Son, in whom I have redemption even the forgiveness of sins. Lord, You have given me all things that pertain to life and godliness; so make me complete in You. As I seek You with my whole heart, I will find You and as I delight in You, put Your desires in my heart. Lord, You created my sexuality and I am asking You to keep it until Your will is fulfilled in my life, so I commit it to You. For I know that You are able to keep that which I have committed to You until that day. Lord, I am trusting Your plan for my life and rejoice knowing that it will come to full fruition, thank You for doing this, in the name of Jesus Christ, my Lord, Amen.

Ethlyn Ottley Farrell

STRENGTH TO STAND IN ADVERSITY

Father God, I come to You because You are my refuge and strength, a very present help in time of trouble. You said in Your word when I am weak then I am strong so I have come in faith believing what You said; for my strength is not in me but in the finish work of Jesus Christ. Lord, strengthen me with Your might by your Spirit in my inner man that Christ may dwell in my heart by faith, and that I being rooted and grounded in love, may be able to comprehend with all saints what is the breadth, and length, and depth, and height; and know the love of God which passes knowledge, that I maybe filled with the fullness of God. Father, teach me how to be strong in You and in the power of Your might. Father, as I put on the whole armor of God, I thank You that I am able to stand against the wiles of the devil. For we do not wrestle against flesh and blood, but against principalities, against powers, against the rulers of the darkness of this age, against spiritual hosts of wickedness in the heavenly places. Therefore, I take up the whole armour of God, that I may be able to withstand in the evil day and having done all, to stand. Stand therefore, having girded my waist with truth, having put on the breastplate of righteousness, and having shod my feet with the preparation of the gospel of peace; above all, taking the shield of faith with which I am able to quench all the fiery darts of the wicked one. Lord, I put on Your helmet of salvation, and the sword of the Spirit, which is the word of God; praying always with all prayer and supplication in the Spirit, being watchful to this end with all perseverance and supplication for all the saints— and for me, that utterance may be given to me, that I may open my mouth boldly to make known the mystery of the gospel for which I am an ambassador in chains;

that in it I may speak boldly, as I ought to speak.

Father, as I stand in Your strength and power, I stand against every attack of the enemy. Everything that attempts to divert, mislead, or confuse me, I break every chain and cut them asunder. I declare that they are permanently destroyed never to be joined again. For the weapons of our warfare are not carnal but mighty in God for the pulling down of strongholds, casting down arguments and every high thing that exalts itself against the knowledge of God, bringing every thought into captivity to the obedience of Christ, and being ready to punish all disobedience when your obedience is fulfilled.

Now unto Him that is able to do exceeding abundantly above all that we ask or think according to the power that works in us. Father, because you are at work within me, I thank You for infusing me with Your divine and supernatural strength. Help me to stand in Your strength, power and the faith that I have in You, for this is the victory that overcomes the world even my faith. Thank You for Your strength being manifested in my life, in the name of the Lord Jesus Christ, Amen.

Ethlyn Ottley Farrell

TRAVELING MERCIES

Father God, I come to You on behalf of _____ and ask as _____ travel to give _____traveling mercies as _____ travel to his/her destination. Lord, I thank You that _____ steps are ordered by You. Therefore, I thank You in advance that _____ will arrive safely to his/her destination. I thank You that Your angels are encamped around _____ and are watching over him/her. I thank You that the mode of transportation _____ is taking will operate and function as it was designed to do. I thank You that there are no mechanical malfunctions or hindering obstacles in _____pathway. I thank You that the highways, byways, airways, and waterways are watched over by You. You see every path; therefore, You will keep _____ on track. If there is something that _____cannot see while traveling, You will allow _____ to see or take a detour. I thank You that _____ is covered by the Blood of Jesus, and because of this no hurt, harm or danger will come nigh to _____. I thank You that there will be no human error and no human threat. I thank You that _____ arrives at his/her destination safely and peacefully, in Jesus name Amen.

Preparing for Surgery

Father God, as we come before Your throne bringing _____ who needs healing. _____ has chosen the path of medical science. As _____ is scheduled for surgery, give him/her peace and remind him/her that You will never leave nor forsake him/her. I take authority over the spirit of fear, worry, stress and anxiety, I command it to go from _____ now in Jesus name. I command every contrary thought that is contradictory to Your word to evaporate from his/her mind. Lord, I thank You, Father, for guiding the doctor's hands giving them wisdom, foresight and insight, as You guide their hands as they do this procedure. Let every process be done with exceptional skill and innovative wisdom. Let every test results come out with a good report in the name of Jesus, for we believe the report of the Lord. We give You thanks in advance for doing it, for by your stripes _____ is healed. We thank You that your best for _____ is that we prosper and be in health even as our souls prosper. We thank You in advance for bringing _____ through surgery successfully. We declare that _____ will experience a speedy full recovery. There will be no complications, infections or setbacks. Thank You, Lord, that all of Your promises are yes and amen, for You watch over Your word to perform it, in Jesus name, Amen.

Ethlyn Ottley Farrell

WALKING INTO VICTORY

Father, I come before You this day boldly because I am in need of Your grace and mercy. You know and understand all things, for You are the Eternal God, the Everlasting Father, the All-Knowing, and All-Wise God. You see everything and You are everywhere. There's no searching of Your understanding. Your understanding is infinite. I am asking You to help me to trust in You with all of my heart and lean not on my own understanding but in all my ways acknowledge You, and You will direct my path. The things I had planned for my life has fallen apart and the counsel I received led me in the wrong way. Lord, I now know Your way is not only a better way, but it is the right way. Lead me in the path of righteousness for Your namesake.

You said that I should not be anxious for nothing but in everything by prayer and supplication with thanksgiving let my requests be known to You. So I present my request to You as I shake off this spirit of defeat, frustration, and heaviness; I counteract it with the garment of praise. Rejoice in You, and again I rejoice. I choose to walk into Your divine, ordained, planned victory for me. I take authority over anxiety, fear, worry and everything that comes against my soul. I command everything that stands in opposition to victory to DIE NOW, in the name of Jesus. I walk out by faith into victory, for this is the victory that overcomes the world even my faith, and I overcome by the blood of the lamb and the word of my testimony. The Word that You have spoken is spirit and life, I receive that life now and declare, thanks be to God, who always gives me the victory through my Lord Jesus Christ, in the name of Jesus, Amen.

Prayers That Touch Heaven And Change Earth

MEN AFFIRMING MEN

Father, we come to You praying over the men that you have called out to serve You for such a time as this. Lord open their eyes so that they see themselves as the new creatures that they are in Christ. Position them in the place that you have ordained for them to occupy in this season of their lives. As they stand in the place of headship, mentorship and leadership in their homes, marketplaces, workplaces and churches. Give them wisdom, understanding and knowledge as they lead their families, co-workers, friends and mentees in love with peace. Send them forth as mighty men of valor blazing a trail in this generation as they leave the mark of Christ on other men. Allow them to influence men with the gospel of the Lord Jesus Christ while bringing change with impact to other men as they speak forth your word in their daily lives and activities. Give them the words to reach and bring deliverance to men who are bound and ravished by the effects of drugs, gangs, alcohol, pornography, adultery, anger, depression, mental illness, poor self-image, hatred, violence, abuse, low self-esteem, workaholism, gender identity issues and low self-worth; as the give them hope while sharing their faith in Christ, the hope of glory. Let their testimonies be the voice that shows Your light and power that opens the doors for them to relate to where they are. As they share the love of God that sets them free to live in freedom and walk away from bondage into victory. May this be the bond that helps them to pull others to safety as they represent You, as men after your own heart. Let their words affirm that men can live for God victoriously as they stand up for the word of truth on the home front, in the marketplace, classroom and board- room, or wherever they go.

Father, thank You that they are men, who love their wives, fathers who discipline their children, and leaders in their community. Give them visions for their homes, and the ability and power to carry them out Your assignment for their lives. Let them be the sample and ensample for their family and community. Let their wives and children call them blessed as they are a blessing to them. Father, may their identity be wrap up in You as You affirm them in the name of Jesus Christ, Amen.

WARFARE PRAYER

Father God, in the name of Jesus, I pray for_____. I take authority over every feeling of frustration, discouragement, self-pity, depression, anxiety, worry, revenge, anger, animosity, un-forgiveness, negative thoughts, and stress that_____is encountering or experiencing, supernaturally ambush every one of them in the name of Jesus. All nightmares, evil dreams, tormenting hallucinations, suicidal attacks and subconscious covert battles are rendered powerless and ineffective. Divinely destruct every fortress erected in the mind of_____ by the enemy. Every weapon formed against_____seen and unseen is demolished and becomes as dust in the name of Jesus Christ. I command every attack of the enemy to come to nought, as confusion infiltrate, derail and consume his troops. As they attack and fight against each other to destroy one another. I reroute, extinguish and snuff out every fiery dart that is sent against and declare that they must fall to the ground and disintegrate in the name of Jesus Christ. Any attempt to counterattack or reformation of the enemy attack suffers backlash.

_____ stands in the authority that is_____as a believer of Jesus Christ. I thank You that You are fighting for_____ because the battle is Yours and therefore the victory is_____. I thank You, Father God, that_____will cast all his/her cares upon You because You care for_____watchfully and affectionately; order_____footsteps today and show_____the way to go, give_____favor with man as_____have with You; help to keep his/her eyes on Jesus, who is the author and finisher of_____faith. Thank You for the victory in the name of Jesus Christ, Amen.

Ethlyn Ottley Farrell

WARFARE PRAYER FOR THE FIVE-FOLD MINISTRY: APOSTLES, PROPHETS, EVANGELISTS, PASTORS AND TEACHERS.

Father, we come to You lifting up those call to the Five-Fold ministry. As we stand in the gap for them, we take authority over every attack of the enemy that has been launched. We declare war on every tactic, scheme, and battle plan that he has put into action, we interrupt and destroy it, in the name of Jesus. We call out and expose to the light of your word every spirit of depression, despair, self-pity, suicide, deception, seduction, lust, dissatisfaction, addiction, manipulation, confusion and entrapment, and the like that has been assigned to them for their destruction and demise. We declare access denied. We break every chain and mind-controlling agent that has bound them to this slavery in the name of Jesus. We come against every and any stronghold that have ensnared them or is pursuing them in ancestral, inherited, familiar patterns and habits that create soul ties linked to adultery, fornication, sexual addictions and any form abuse of themselves or with mankind such as, drug addiction, alcoholism, pornography prescription drugs, homosexuality and any kind of perversion not known to man but known to God. We sever every tie and declare it burnt up by the fire of the Holy Spirit. We break every path and access points used by familiar spirits from ancestral, generational or family habits from the past over them. We call out every attack and plan of the enemy and declare them null void and ineffective. We command every pathway to them and neo-pathway to their souls closed, eradicated, undetectable and burnt; we declare it totally inaccessible and erased never to be found in the spirit realm again. Every desire that's not of God is cast down in the name of Jesus. Every relationship in which the enemy is able to access and influence them with evil is severed never to be realigned or reestablished, revisited, or reopened. We intercede for those seduced or enslaved to occult practices, call or consult psychics, astrological predictions, mediums, witches or witchdoctors, Father, deliver them. Let their desire be to seek You and remind them that You are a jealous God. We break down the networks of communication, spyware, and hackers in the realm of the spirit and render any forced downloads or falsely attained documents unreachable, unreadable, and unattainable in the name of Jesus. Every spirit wife or husband, witch or warlock masquerading as a saint be exposed and destroyed in the name of Jesus. Anything eaten drunk or entered into their systems which have been fixed, sent, dressed or set for their harm, to destroy their health or mind and cause premature death, be vomited and purged from their system by the blood of Jesus.

You said that they would eat deadly things and it will not harm them, and we believe You. Every barrier and hindrance that is stopping them from fulfilling the call that You have placed on their lives we command it to break in the name of Jesus. We stand on Your word and authority You have given us for You have given us the authority to tread on serpents and scorpions and all the works of the enemy and nothing by any means shall harm us. We cover them in and with the blood of Jesus and pray a hedge of protection around them that no evil will come nigh them or their dwelling. They will live in peaceable houses, secure habitations, and quiet resting places. We surround them with our faith and love, and pray a prayer wall of protection around them, as we are obedient to pray for our leaders in the Five-Fold ministry, in the name of the Lord Jesus Christ, Amen.

Ethlyn Ottley Farrell

WARFARE PRAYER FOR GENERATIONAL CONTROLLING SPIRITS

Father, I come to you bringing _____ (state problem or issue) to You and I lift it up; l cover _____ with the blood of Jesus and put a hedge of protection around it in the name of Jesus. I take authority over every controlling, familiar, generational spirit and I break the influence and hold it has over _____ in the name of Jesus. I break down every stronghold and expose every lying, treacherous, wicked spirit of deceit. I command you to be quiet and stop speaking lies into _____ minds, in the name of Jesus. Father, open the eyes of _____ to the truth about their enemies and help _____ to cut off every hindering thing, destructive habit, seen and unseen obstacles from _____. Cause every contact, contract, or covenant with a person or spirit that speaks contrary to Your will to be disconnected and come to an end. Dissolve every partnership with the enemy and let them recognize his schemes of division, confusion and strife as You eradicate all spyware, virus and bugs from the network of _____ lives. Give _____ a fresh perspective of Your saving grace and Your mercy that is new every day.

Open their ears so that they hear Your voice and know Your voice and the voice of the stranger they do not follow. Help them to speak forth life as they become a force to be reckoned with, as they battle the enemy of their _____. Remind them that two is better than one and bring agreement to the _____. Let the love that is poured into their hearts by the Holy Spirit come forth as they walk in love, practice love and speak the truth in love. Cause Your wisdom to be downloaded in their minds as they ask you For wisdom in _____ Restore and refresh their hope in the plan that You have made for_____. Father, let every desire that is in line and agreement with Your will be established in their lives on earth as it is in heaven in the name of the Lord Jesus Christ, Amen.

Ethlyn Ottley Farrell

WARFARE PRAYER FOR EMOTIONAL DISTRESS

Father God, I bring _____ to You. As this sabotage has been launched, I pray that You remove every negative residual effect of the encounter with the enemy and the memories of the past. Eradicate every thought, emotion, and feeling that the enemy has resurrected to cause_____ to fall into a place of despair, depression, failure and distress. I rebuke the spirit of depression, torment, and deception. I command them to stop their assault against the mind of _____ in the name of Jesus. I give you notice devil that when the enemy comes in like a flood, the Spirit of the Lord lifts up a standard against you. Father give _____ peace and wisdom to recognize, navigate, and destroy the mazes, snares, and traps of the enemy. Help _____ to guard his/her heart, mind and emotion as he/she surrender to Your unconditional love. Heal all the painful memories and broken dreams in _____ life, for You are the Lord God that heals. Lord, You are not a man that You should lie nor the son of man that You should repent; if You said it You will do it and if You promised it You will make it good. Father, I thank You for healing all of the wounds and restoring _____ to health. Infuse _____ with hope where it seems hopeless through Jesus Christ the hope of glory. Reassuring ____ that You have plans for his/her life to give _____ a hope and a future to bring him/her to an expected end. Restore to _____ a peace of mind. As _____ release every negative or harmful thought that comes to _____ mind. By Your delegated authority that You gave to _____ cast it down and plead the Blood of Jesus over _____ thoughts. We thank that Your are bringing every thought into captivity; _____ is no longer enslaved to the bondservant, _____ is free because Your word says who the Son sets free, he is free indeed, in Jesus name, Amen.

Ethlyn Ottley Farrell

Warring Against Wrong Attitudes

Father, we come before You with our hearts open to You. Search us, O' God, and know our hearts, try us and know our thoughts and see if there is any evil in us, remove it and lead us in Your way everlasting. Expose every action, attitude or behavior that leads us to the path of offense, division, frustration, and into a cycle of destructive thinking that takes us on a course of bad thoughts and wrong attitudes. Allow us to be sensitive to Your Spirit as You give us the revelation to discern which thoughts are ours and to recognize the attack of the enemy through our thought life. Cleanse us from every demonic influence that creates thoughts and impressions that infect our attitudes and deliver us from their influence. We come against the trap of the enemy that he has set to harness the mind, will and emotions and break every stronghold that he has built to hide in and inhabit in the name of Jesus. We take authority over every plan of the enemy and command every stronghold to crumble and be grounded into ashes and be blown away in the wind never to be found again in the spiritual or natural realm. Bring deliverance to our minds, will, and emotions as You sent Your word to heal us and deliver us from all our destructions. Help us to extinguish every thought pattern, attitude or habit that contradicts and stops us from walking in newness of life. We present our bodies as a living sacrifice, holy and acceptable to You which is our reasonable service and are not conformed to this world but transform by the renewing of our minds; let this mind be in us that was also in Christ Jesus that even though He was equal with God, He did not count it as anything but humbled Himself as a man even to death on the cross. Lord, help us to bring our thoughts under the scrutiny of Your word for it is a lamp to our feet and a light to our path. Cleanse us with truth; Your word is truth. Let Your word be the transforming agent to bring us nigh unto you as You wash us with the washing of the water of Your word. Let every negative thought be removed as You restore our souls and bring every thought into obedience to the Lord Jesus Christ. We declare total deliverance in the name of Jesus, Amen.

Ethlyn Ottley Farrell

WARFARE PRAYER FOR CHILDREN

Lord, we come to you on the behalf of all the children of the world - the next generation. The enemy has declared war on them, but we know that you have a plan and purpose for their very existence. Your word says that You are looking for one to stand in the gap and make up the hedge, so we are here to be the one. We cover them with the blood of Jesus and surround them with our faith and love. We take authority over every attack, strategy and plan of the enemy. We command him to stop and abort every assignment against them. We capture and annihilate every fiery dart, missile and weapon sent for his or her untimely and premature death. Every assigned and premeditated act of violence sent out against them from the natural or spirit realm must cease in the name of Jesus. We arrest the spirit of suicide, murder, assassination, gang induction and initiation that has been assigned to their lives to bring death and destruction. We cut off every point of access to their spirit, soul and bodies that have been invaded by familiar spirits and demonic influences. We come against the spirit of rebellion, religion, rejection, machoism, confusion and fear, we breakdown the strongholds over their minds, of mind control, new age thinking and melancholy. We breakdown the altars of the lust of the flesh, the lust of the eyes and the pride of life and scatter everything that feed these things that's not of You. Lord, extend your arms of mercy and love to them. Let Your grace by faith save them from the path of the enemy and pull them into the path of Your salvation. Fill them with the word and make them skillful in the use of it, which is the sword of the Spirit. Make them proficient and fervent in prayer. Raise them up to be the generation of warriors that is confident in Your power to destroy the strongholds of the enemy and expose the deception of his power. Let them experience deliverance, and victory as they pursue, overtake and annihilate every plan of the enemy. Use them to proclaim the gospel and demonstrate it; as they show forth Your light, in their generation, in the name of the Lord Jesus Christ, Amen.

Ethlyn Ottley Farrell

Prayer Against Human Trafficking

Father, I come and bring before You the harvesting of human beings or human trafficking which is slavery. Lord, we ask You to intervene divinely and stop these unspeakable atrocities that are being done to and carried out against mankind all over the world. Open the eyes of those in authority to this crime, give them wisdom and insight to help them to bring it to an end and the perpetrators to justice, in the name of Jesus. Expose every secret meeting place, clandestine plot and inhumane plan to lure, kidnap and capture their innocent, unsuspecting victims. Let this cycle of destruction and degradation be broken down in the name of Jesus. Deliver those on whom this crime has been committed from abuse of every kind, low self-esteem; every form of addiction, self-hatred, and drug dependencies. Set them free in spirit, soul and body. Give them amnesia so that they forget the inhumane acts that have been done to them. Heal and save them as only You can. Infiltrate the organizations of the perpetrators of this horrific practice with anointed vessels assigned to rescue the victims of this crime. Give them strategies, wisdom and courage to follow through with your divine plan. Step up ambushments, and give them Your divine help spiritually and naturally for those who are agents of rescue. Allow them to get the victims to a place of safety, without the threat of recapture or retaliation, where they can receive help, hope, and healing for total restoration, soundness of mind and peace. May they encounter your unconditional love that is filled with your transforming and delivering power as they meet and accept Jesus as Lord and Savior. Father, as they recover from the enemy plan of destruction and have experienced Your supernatural power of healing, restoration, and deliverance, help them to forgive themselves as well as the captives and perpetrators of these crimes and terrible acts. Deposit within them hearts of compassion to allow them to empathize with others. Use their stories as testimonies of Your divine ability to bring freedom to those in impossible, difficult and disastrous situations and circumstances. Raise them up to minister life to others as prayer warriors, Intercessors, anointed advocates and agents of freedom and deliverance that will help those who suffers from the same or similar fate. May Your kingdom come, and Your will be done on earth as it is in heaven in the name of the Lord Jesus Christ, Amen.

HEALING

Father, You are the Lord God that heals and You promised to heal all my wounds and restore me to health. Lord, I ask You to heal me from_____in the name of Jesus. I declare Your word this day, for You said that if I attend to Your word, and incline my ears to Your sayings, and do not let them depart from my eyes, but keep it in the midst of my heart that they will be life to me who have found it and health and healing to all my flesh. Lord, You said that healing is the children's bread. The effective, fervent prayer of a righteous man avails much, and that when we seek You with all of our heart, You will be found. Lord, You said Ask, and it will be given to You; seek, and You will find; knock, and it will be opened to You. For everyone who asks receives, and he who seeks finds, and to him who knocks it will be opened.

Lord, You were wounded for my transgressions, bruised for my iniquities, the chastisement of my peace was upon You, and by Your stripes, I am healed; for the self-same spirit that raised Jesus from the dead lives within me, and that self-same Spirit quickens, makes alive my mortal body. I declare that every organ, muscle, and cell, functions in perfection to which it was created to function. Everything in my body is in alignment with the word of God. I declare that my blood pressure, blood sugar, and cholesterol levels are normal. Lord Jesus, You died and rose with all power, and I am accepted in the Beloved; therefore, I claim and receive my healing. I thank You for Jesus righteousness, and that I am the righteousness of God in Christ. Lord, You have declared in Your word that if I serve You that You would bless my bread and water and take sickness out of the midst of thee; I receive my healing by faith. I thank You for allyour promises that are yes and amen. You that spared not Your own Son but delivered Him up for us all, how shall You not with Him freely give us all things? Your best for me is; beloved above all things I wish that thou would prosper and be in health even as thy soul prospers. Lord, You have promised that You will never leave me nor forsake me and You will not withhold any good thing from me who walk uprightly. Father, I am gratefully thankful for Your loving kindness and tender mercies that You have poured into my life and I thank You in advance that I receive divine health in the name of the Lord Jesus Christ, Amen.

Ethlyn Ottley Farrell

HEALING FOR VICTIMS OF INCEST

Father God, I come to you asking You to help me to deal with the effects of being a victim of incest by a family member or close friend. Lord, I desire to be cleanse and washed by Your word and blood anew. You said that whatsoever I desire when I pray, believe I receive it, and I will have it.

I run to You knowing that You love me and You can make me whole. As a result of this act, I ask You to deliver me from promiscuity, homosexuality, bitterness, low esteem, self-hatred, suicide, emotional and mental distress. Erase every trace of self-pity with its victim mentality that the enemy uses as a gateway to depression. Engage me as I transform and renew my mind by Your word. Father, make me whole again as You infuse my mind with supernatural hope. Give me strength and build resistance inside of me so that I don't allow this horrific event to take me into captivity and build a stronghold in my life. Don't let this be the window from where I view my life, but let this be a catalyst to push me into living a blessed, prosperous and fruitful life. Use this that the enemy meant for bad and turn it around for good. As I let my light so shine before men that they may see my good works and glorify my Father which is in heaven, use me as an advocate for others who have gone through this ordeal. Protect them from anger, rejection and abuse when they reveal to the parent, guardian, or custodian of the incestuous act; along with the accusations and lies that they brought it on themselves or when the perpetrator is believed and protected and they are not. Deliver those who are allowed to be continually victimized because of fear, financial dependency, warp thinking and weird traditions. Expose this secret act of shame and horrific violation that is hidden by many families for generations and bring healing to them, in the name of Jesus. Father, I know that Your word says that all things work together for good to those who love You and are called according to Your purpose. Direct my eyes that I would see the good even in this, so I may not be tormented. Fear has torment, but I do not fear for You are with me, and I am not dismayed for You are my God, You will help me, strengthen me and uphold me with the right hand of Your righteousness. Lord, I thank You that there is no condemnation to those who are in Christ; if my heart condemns me, You are greater than my heart and You know all things; if my heart condemns me not, I have confidence in You.

Help me to forgive the perpetrator of this act, even as God for Christ sake has forgiven me. Teach me how to pray for him/her, because you said in Your word for us to pray for our enemy. I pray for his/her deliverance from this perversion so that he/she may not do this to another person. I know that nothing is too difficult for You, and I ask that You would give me the grace to love this person in spite of what they did to me. You said that perfect love cast out all fear, as you love me, I am able to love those who harm me. I thank You that You are depositing within me the ability to trust again and to exercise wisdom in how I relate to others.

I receive Your healing for all the residual effects of incest and any of its long-term effects. I declare that I am healed; for I overcome by the blood of the Lamb and the word of my testimony in, the name of the Lord Jesus Christ, Amen.

Ethlyn Ottley Farrell

HEALING FOR VICTIMS OF RAPE

Father, I come to You because You love me unconditionally and I ask You to help me to recover from the violence of rape that has affected my life in numerous ways. Release me from being perpetually a victim and the bondage of every trap that the enemy has laid for me, in the name of Jesus. Nothing is hidden from You and all things are open to the eyes of Him with whom I have to do. Expose every lie about this crime that is established in society and allow it to be viewed as the act of violence that it is. Educate the justice system to effectively deal with this crime as they persecute the criminal without putting the victim on trial. Give them wisdom with divine strategies to protect the victim from reliving the ordeal again and again. Release those who are afraid to tell of their victimization from reoccurring dreams, emotional and mental challenges. Erase all the painful memories and the torment from the fear in their soul; mind, will and emotions. Let me be free from the past stigma, public humiliation, and embarrassment; let my future become what you have planned for me, in the name of Jesus. For You have declared in Your word that You have a plan for me, for good and not evil, to give me a hope and a future, an expected end. Father God, heal me so that I can be free from all the guilt, condemnation and anxiety that has plagued me in the daytime and in my sleep by the reoccurring nightmares from this violation in my life. You are the Lord God that heals me, and I know that what You have promised You are able to perform. Give me sweet restorative sleep, as the power of Your love heals my inner most being. As I present this petition before You, deposit in my heart and mind Your peace that passes all understanding that will keep my heart and mind in Christ Jesus. Your love in me creates the ability to-help me to forgive the perpetrator of this terrible act against me and release him so that I can walk in the freedom that You have provided for me. As Your love sets me free, it releases within me the ability to forgive myself and releases me from the blame and shame of this act of rape. Lord, I know that nothing is too difficult for You and healing is the children bread: I accept and believe Your word. I trust in You, my Lord Jehovah, for in You is everlasting strength. I thank You for restoring everything that has been stolen from me, in the name of the Lord Jesus Christ, Amen

Ethlyn Ottley Farrell

HEALING FOR VICTIMS OF MOLESTATION

Father, we bring _____ to You, who has been molested/ is a victim of molestation. As we lift up our voices on_____ behalf, we ask You to deliver_____ from the guilt, shame, and embarrassment along with every thought of torment that the enemy would use to make _____ feel that it was their fault. Although _____ decision to come forward and expose this situation may have resulted in divorce, incarceration, alienation or estrangement of a family member. Lord, give them the assurance and let them realize that they did the right thing. Erase every familiar track and pathway in their minds that the enemy has used as an access point of torment to their soul, in the name of Jesus. May the same power that raised Jesus from the dead, bring healing to _____ as it flows from the top of their heads to the soles of their feet, You heal all their wounds and restore them to health. Release Your healing power to help _____ to forgive themselves; let it overflow to forgive the person that the enemy used to carry out this act, even as God for our sake has forgiven them. In their releasing of them, may they experience total healing and deliverance in every area of hurt, pain and distress; for whom the Son has set free, is free indeed. You are a God of mercy, grace, and restoration, remind _____ that Your plan and will be established in _____ life. Turn around all that the enemy had meant for bad for good in the name of the Lord Jesus Christ, Amen.

HEALING FOR MEN WHO GREW UP WITHOUT A FATHER

Father God, we are coming before You lifting up these men who are searching for their identity and wholeness. Lord, they have wrapped themselves up in a coat of machoism and hardness, deliver them and set them free from the fear and opinion of men, in the name of Jesus. You are the Father of all. Lord, I ask You to help them to identify with Your love; set them free from the haunting thoughts of their father's rejection, abandonment and the denial of their existence, even of their paternity, in the name of Jesus. Allow Your healing power to flow into them and destroy every feeling of anger, rejection, self-hatred, internal anguish, abuse, addictive behaviors, self-destructive habits and brokenness that they use as a place to hide the pain and torment inside of their heart and soul; heal all their wounds and restore them to health. Let them know that You love them unconditionally, and You did not come into the world to condemn the world but to save it. Father, I ask You to tear down the wall of isolation that they have built around themselves; place within them a heart of flesh, and replace the heart of stone. Help them to forgive their fathers even as God for Christ sake has forgiven them. We take authority over every attack of the enemy and destroy every plan, assignment, and strategy he has crafted in their lives. We break the powers of darkness over their minds and speak forth liberty over them. Lord, teach them how to be fathers with their children. Let them glean from their heavenly Father for identity, purpose, and wisdom. Restore everything in their lives to include their identity, in the name of Jesus, Amen.

Ethlyn Ottley Farrell

Healing for those Struggling with their Sexual Identity

Father, You are a God of mercy forgiveness and grace; there is nothing too hard for You. Lord, we come before Your throne responding to Your invitation. For we know that what's impossible with us is possible with You. We bring before You those who are struggling with their sexuality. Lord, You created us male and female; You made us in your image then declared it good. We know that You, Lord, don't make mistakes. Dear Father, we ask that You heal whatever issue or incident that has caused this mindset to attached itself to_____. We pull down every stronghold of the enemy that has infiltrated their minds, will and emotions. Replace it with the truth of Your word, for Your word is truth.

Break every generational, ancestral and familiar assignment that has influenced this erroneous lifestyle. We stand against the onslaught, bombardment or infiltration upon our young people to persuade them this is normal. We come against the purposeful attack on the next generations and interrupt the plans of the enemy. We speak confusion to his plan and declare when the enemy comes in like a flood the Spirit of the Lord lifts up a standard. Heal_____mind from the lies of deception that society has fed them through the media, social media, and all other sources. Erase every lie of the enemy that has been spoken over their lives by themselves or others. Heal_____ spirit, soul and body then they will be healed. For what is impossible with us is possible with you. Holy Father draw them by the power of the Holy Spirit, and let them encounter Your unconditional love that draws men to repentance. This is the confidence we have in You, that, if we ask anything according to Your will, You hear us, and if we know that You hear us we have the petitions we desire of You.

Lord thank You for divinely intervening in this, in the name of the Lord Jesus Christ, Amen.

Ethlyn Ottley Farrell

Healing for the Broken Heart

Father God, I come to You because I know that You love me unconditionally and that You heal broken hearts. Lord, I do not know which way to turn, but I believe Your word. You said that You would never leave me or forsake me. I am depending on You to do what You say You will do. Lord, Your word is forever settled in heaven, and I believe Your word. Heal all of my wounds and restore me to health for You are the Lord God that healeth thee.

I take authority over every attack of the enemy that comes against my mind, will and emotions. I speak to self-pity, confusion, depression, and discouragement to be gone. I command you, Satan to back up off of me in the name of Jesus. For God gave me authority to tread upon serpents and scorpions and all the power of the enemy and nothing by any means shall harm me. I stand on Your word, knowing that You are backing me up, for You watch over Your word to perform it.

Thank You, Father, that You sent Your word to heal me and deliver me from all my destruction. For You were wounded for my transgressions, bruised for my iniquities, the chastisement of my peace was upon You, and by Your stripes, I am healed. You promise to heal my broken heart, and I know You will; for You are not a man that You should lie nor the son of man that You should repent. If You said it, You will do it. If You promise it, You will make it good.

Lord Your word says the steps of a good man are ordered of the Lord, set my feet on a plain path, for my steps are ordered of You. I trust in Your plan for my life. You are my hope. Thank You Lord that Jesus is the hope of glory. Thank You for healing me in the name of the Lord Jesus Christ, Amen.

HEALING FOR CHILDREN REJECTED BY PARENTS

Father God, I come to You asking for Your help with this issue of not being loved or wanted by my parents. Lord Jesus, because You were rejected by men also, You can associate with the pain that I have experienced. Lord, help me to first forgive them because even though I was not their plan; l am Your plan. Help me to release the anger, hurt, and rejection that the enemy has used to try to consume me. You are the Lord that heals and You have promised to heal all of our wounds and restore us to health. Remove all of the defenses, desires and destructive habits that lead me to explore lifestyles of perversion. I come against every addictive spirit of drugs alcohol and sex, every spirit of low self-esteem or wrong self-image. For You have given me the power to tread on serpents and scorpions and over all the power of the enemy and nothing by any means will harm me. Father, I ask You to have mercy on me and help me to identify with You as the Father of all. Allow me to experience Your healing power within me and let everything that is not of You die totally in the name of Jesus. So that I may receive the full impact of Your love for me, as Your child. Lord, You said that You that spared not Your own son; but delivered Him up for us all, how shall You not with Him give us all things. Give me Your peace that passes all understanding as I present this petition before You. Thank You for doing it, in the name of the Lord Jesus Christ, Amen.

Ethlyn Ottley Farrell

CHILDBEARING DIFFICULTY CONCEIVING BARRENNESS

Father God, I come to You because Your ears are open to my prayers and You hear my cry. This is the confidence that I have in You, that if I ask You anything according to Your will, You hear me and if I know that You hear me, then I know I have the petitions that I desire of You. So now Father, I ask You in the name of Jesus, to open my womb that I can conceive and bring forth a baby/children. You said that children are a blessing of the Lord the fruit of the womb Your reward. Happy is the man that has his quiver full; his wife will be a fruitful vine at the side of His house, and His children liked olive plants around His table. Now Father, as You showed Your hand when Hannah cried out to You, show me Your mercy and compassion. Father, You said a barren womb is never satisfied. And I know that You will not withhold anything from those who walk uprightly. Thank You for my good things, my children, in the name of Jesus.

Now, I speak to my body and my husband's body; I command them to align with the word of God. Reproductive organs function in the perfection that you were created to function. Any missing tubes or ovaries, we speak into you to be formed by God's creative power in the name of Jesus. Sperm count, increase to the maximum level in the name of Jesus. Endometriosis, any blockage or deformities or defects, disappear in the name of Jesus. Under developed reproductive cells, be developed and mature right now.

I decree and declare that any witchcraft, black magic, voodoo or any other form of darkness from the realm of the enemy is rendered powerless. No more stress, spontaneous abortion, miscarriages or delays, in the name of Jesus.

Lord, Your Word said Behold, I give unto your power to tread on serpents and scorpions, and over all the power of the enemy: and nothing shall by any means hurt you.

Father God, I have a more sure word of prophecy which is Your word and Your promises are yea and amen.

Now Father God, just as You did for Abraham and Sarah, do now for me because in Your kingdom there is no biological clock. You quicken the dead and call those things that be not as though they are; the self-same Spirit that raised Jesus from the dead quickens my mortal body because the same Spirit dwells in Me. Father, thank You for watching over Your Word to perform it.

Thank You for Your answer to this prayer, and I will not forget to give You all the glory, honor and praise. Thank You for the miracle in advance, in the name of the Lord Jesus Christ, Amen.

Ethlyn Ottley Farrell

SHIFTING THE ATMOSPHERE

Lord, we worship You and adore You and bless Your Holy name. We cover this place with the blood of Jesus and take authority over every spirit of confusion, discord, jealousy, envy, strife, backbiting, gossip, and division; for You, Lord, gave us power to tread on serpents and scorpions and over all the powers of the enemy and nothing by any means shall harm us. We speak to every demonic atmospheric influence in this place; we ban and banish them from operating in this atmosphere in the name of Jesus. We come against the spirit of rebellion, control, manipulation and every familiar spirit that tries to operate against us. We command them to leave this place in the name of Jesus. We invite You, Holy Spirit to come and dwell in our midst. To lead and guide us into all truth, bring to our remembrance those things that Jesus said and show us that which is to come. Lord, we honor and glorify You and thank You that You inhabit the praises of Your people. Pour forth the oil of Your presence, power, glory and fire on us as we seek You with our whole heart. We bless, magnify, and adore You because You are the wonderful, magnificent King of kings and Lord of lords. Hallelujah to Your name! It's not by might, not by power but by Your Spirit. You said where two or three are gathered in Your name You are here in our midst. Father, cause Your presence to fill this place. Let the glory of the latter house be greater than the former house. Shift this atmosphere as Your Kingdom come, and Your will be done on earth as it is in heaven. Cause Your presence to fill this place to bless Your people and as a result release Your power to heal physically, emotionally and spiritually.

Hallelujah! Hallelujah! Hallelujah! May Your people be-transformed by Your glory. We exalt you Almighty God and praise Your Holy name. We appreciate Your presence and power as we are healed, restored and revived in this atmosphere, in the name of the Lord Jesus Christ, Amen.

Ethlyn Ottley Farrell

Prayer for Israel

Father God, we lift up to You the nation of Israel and pray for this holy nation of God. We ask You to bless, protect and surround this nation with a wall of peace and heal this war-torn place in the name of Jesus. As You strategically position watchmen on the wall to recognize the attacks of the enemy, rescue them and show them your mercy. Supernaturally intercept, ambush and destroy every plan, trap and attack of the enemy spiritually and naturally on this country, in the name of Jesus. You said that You will bless those who bless Israel, so we bless Israel and her people. Lord, allow Your chosen people to embrace Your Son the Lord Jesus Christ as their Messiah, along with the new covenant that is written in Your blood. Erase from their hearts and mind every intentional plan of deception that has been passed from one generation to another by the traditions of men. As You prosper this city, bring Your people into a relationship with You by acknowledging and accepting Jesus as their Saviour. Lord, let them experience the everlasting covenant through Your unconditional love and goodness that draws men to repentance; for this is the confidence that we have in You that if we ask You anything according to Your will You hear us and if we know that You hear us we have the petitions we desire of You. We thank You for doing it in the name of the Lord Jesus Christ, Amen.

Prayer for Peace in the Countries of the World

Father God, we come to You asking that You intervene in the affairs of men in the countries of the world to bring about peace. Your word says that nation will rise against nation and kingdom against kingdom; that there will be wars and rumors of wars, but the end is not yet. Lord, we know that Your mercy is new every morning and great is Your faithfulness, so we come appealing to You for Your mercy, asking that You would cause peace to come to the countries of the world that have been ravished and destroyed by the conflicts of men and war. Divinely interfere in the battles that are taking innocent lives that are the results of war. Bring an end to the intentional murders and mass murders that are done by suicide bombers, terrorist groups and individuals who are deceived by the lies of the enemy. Interrupt the diabolical plans of the evil leaders of those who are carrying out these acts in the name of Jesus; for when the enemy comes in like a flood the Spirit of the Lord will lift a standard against him.

Allow the gospel to reach those who have not heard it, as You have promised in Your word; that this gospel of the kingdom shall be preached in the whole world as a testimony to all the nations, and then the end will come. So Father bring peace in these countries, protect the missionaries with the blood of Jesus, as they are obedient to Your call and let them eat the good of the land. Give them covert strategies, divine revelation and direction to get the word inside hostile territories. Arm them with supernatural courage and help as they carry out Your plan to take the gospel to all the earth. Let them go out with joy and be led forth with peace as they fulfill Your will on earth, as it is in heaven, in the name of the Lord Jesus Christ, Amen.

PRAYER FOR INTERCESSORS AND PRAYER WARRIORS

Father God, we call upon You for Your Word declares that if I call on You, You will show me great and mighty things that I do not know. This call is on behalf of Intercessors and prayer warriors around the world, those who are called out to be in the birthing room, as well as the boardroom, on the frontline, the wall, and the prayer closet; those in special operations, on covert assignments and upholding the hands of visionaries; those in warfare for families, nations and territories; bringing salvation, healing and deliverance through prayer, vigilant prayer watches and by travailing in intercession. Lord, I ask that You may strengthen them with Your might in their inner man, that Christ may dwell in their hearts by faith, and they being rooted and grounded in Your love may be able to comprehend with all the saints what is the breadth, the length, the depth and height and to know love of God which passes knowledge, and to be filled with the fullness of God. Now unto Him who is able to do exceeding abundantly above all that we can ask or think, accord- ing to His power that is at work within us, to Him be the glory world without end. We declare that no weapon formed against them will prosper and every tongue that rises against them will be condemned; there will be no backlash or retaliation to their prayers. We pray a prayer wall, a hedge of protection and draw a bloodline around them, their families, businesses, and homes, all that concerns them, in the name of Jesus. Every assigned attack, preplanned ambush and covert mission that the enemy has arranged is in disarray, disarmed, and destroyed. All germ warfare, viruses, chronic diseases, reoccurring illnesses sent out to afflict and affect the health of any Intercessors/ prayer warriors is rendered null void and ineffective. We take authority over the spirit of infirmity and command it to be gone; disrupt- ing and dismantling every attack of the enemy, in the name of Jesus. Father, reveal every agent of evil, wickedness, and dark- ness, natural and spiritual, expose their dishonest schemes, plots of manipulation, hearts of hatred and tongues of deceit. Allow every unfriendly friend to be revealed with every ungodly in- tention and imagination to be eradicated, in the name of Jesus. Father, Your word declares, And let us not be weary in well doing: for in due season we shall reap if we faith not. Lord re- energize, restore and resurrect the drive, desire and determination to pray in every intercessor/ prayer warrior that has become weary and abandoned their post, through the power, presence and fire of Your, Holy Spirit. Stir up in _____ by the power of Your love the tenacity to pray through to breakthrough. Re- mind_____ that Your joy is their strength and as_____stay on task restore the joy of their salvation. May the compassion that Jesus possessed be the motivating agent that causes us to pursue in prayer and let joy be the result of every answered prayer. As we remember, that it is not by might, not by power, but by the Spirit and we can do nothing without You, in the name of the Lord Jesus Christ, Amen.

SCRIPTURAL GLOSSARY

1. Prayer for Government

    - 1 Timothy 2:1/2; Isaiah 11:2-4; Proverbs 11:14; Psalms 33:12; 2 Chronicles 7:15 Proverbs 29:2; Matthew 6:14

2. Prayer for Our Church Leaders

    - James 5:16; Isaiah 32:28, 54:17; Ephesians 6:13; Exodus 17:22 Matthew 6:13.

3. Prayer for Marriage: Husbands and Wives

    - Hebrews 4:16; Colossians 3:13; 1 Corinthians 13:4-8; James 1:19,22; Matthew 18:18-19; Joel 2:25; Ephesians 5:22-25; Romans 8:37.

4. Prayer for Marriage

    - Hebrews 13:4; Colossians 3:13; 4:6; Galatians 5:16; Ephesians 5:21-25, 31,4:15; 1 Peter 3:7; Ecclesiastes 4:12; Psalms 34:10; Proverbs 3:6

5. Intimacy in Marriage

- Luke 18:1; Psalms 46:1; Ephesians 4:15, 5:33; 1 John 3:18; 1 Corinthians 7:15; 1 Peter 2:24, 3:7

6. Surviving Divorce

- John 3:16; Malachi 2:16; Mark 11:25; 1 John. 4:18; Psalms 23:6, 51:10; 1 Corinthians 10:4-5; Romans 12:2; Isaiah 53: 4-5; Jeremiah 30:17; Proverbs 3:4-5

7. Prayer for Children

- Psalms 127:3; Colossians 1:10; Matthew 6:33; 18:18; John 16:13,17:17; Ephesians 1:18; Proverbs 22:6; Luke 1:30

8. Prayer for Our School System

- Psalm 138:8; Matthew 6:10; Mark 11:24; Isaiah 55:11; James 1:5; Proverbs 18:1; Romans 4:17

9. Prayer for Families Going Through Separation and Divorce

- Psalms 91; 1; Isaiah 26:4; Matthew 18:18; Luke 10:19; Psalms 34:4; 23:4; Hebrews 12:2

10. Prayer for Forgiving Yourself and Others

- Hebrews 4:16; Mark 11:25; Colossians 3:14; James 1:22

11. Prayer for Rededication for Backslidden Believers

- 1 John 1:9; Revelation 2:4; Matthew 5:6,6:34

12. Prayer of Thanksgiving

- 1 Thessalonians 5:17; Psalms 136:1-3; 103:3; Philippians 4:6; Nehemiah 4:8; Proverbs 10:22; Hebrews 13:15

13. Prayer for Direction

- Psalms 37:23; 138:8; Proverbs 4:18; Matthew 18:18; Jeremiah 29:11

14. Prayer for Wisdom

- James 1:5; 3:17; Proverbs 4: 5; 2 Corinthians 10:5; John 20:27

15. Renewing the Mind

- Philemon 1:6; 1 Corinthians 2:6; Romans 12:1-2; Philippians 4:8

16. Salvation

- Romans 10:9-10

17. Salvation for the Lost

- Psalms 2:8; John 12:32, 9:1; Matthew 18:18, 9:38, 5:6, 6:33

18. Gathering the End Time Harvest

- Matthew 9:31; 2 Peter 3:9; 2 Corinthians 7:10; John 3:17; Proverbs 25:11

19. Greater Works

- John 10:16,27, 14:12,15:15; 2 Tim 2:21; Luke 3:16 Matthew 19:26; Ephesians 6:10-17; Zechariah 4:6; Romans 6:4, 8:14; Galatians 5:16; Hebrews 12:2

20. Having Love One for Another

- Mark 12:31; James 1:22; Romans 5:5; Ephesians 4:15; 1 John 3:18

21. Ministry

- Revelation 3:8,12:11; Psalms 37:23, 43:18; 2 Kings 2:9; Matthew 18:18; John 10:10; Isaiah 11:2-4, 54:17; 2 Tim1: 7; Proverbs 18:1; Ephesians 5:16; Romans 8:14, 5:5; Galatians 5:25; Philippians 4:13; Genesis 22:14; John 10:10; 3 John 2; James 4:10

22. The Five-Fold Ministry

- Luke 18:1; Joshua 1:7; Matthew 22:14, 13:8,18:18; Psalms 138:8; 1 Peter 5:7; Proverbs 3:4-5; Isaiah 26:3; Luke 9:1; Exodus 17:12; Ephesians 5:15; Isaiah 40:28; Romans 8:28; 1 Corinthians 15:57

23. Provision for the Vision

- Habakkuk 2:23; Isaiah 1:19; 1 Peter 5: 7;Philippians 4:6; John 10:10; 1 John 5:14-15; James 1:17; Isaiah 26:3; Psalms 37:3

24. Business

- Genesis 22:14; Philippians 4:19; Isaiah 40:28; James 1:17; 1 Kings 5:18; Luke 6:38; Joshua 1:8

25. Finances

- Philippians 4:19; Luke 6:38; James 1:5; Ephesians 4:1; Proverbs 20:22

26. Knowing God as Our Source

- Philippians 4:19; Numbers 23:19; Psalms 107:20; 2 Timothy 1:7; James 4:7; Romans 8:28; 2 Peter 1:3; 1 Thessalonians 5:17

27. Understanding the Grace of God

- Ephesians 1:27-23, 2:8; Philippians 2:13; Psalms 119:105; Hebrews 4:16; 2 Corinthians 9:8

28. Single Looking for a Mate

- Philippians 4:6; James 1:17; Ephesians 15:25; Matthew 5:6; 18:18; Luke 6:38; Hebrews 4:13; 1 Corinthians 7:9

29. Single and Satisfied

- Psalms 37:5; Proverbs 16:3; Galatians 5:2; Colossians 1:10-14, 2:10; Hebrews 2:17

30. Strength to Stand in Adversity

- Psalms 46:1; 2 Corinthians 13:9; Ephesians 3:16-20, 6:10; 1 John 5:4

31. Traveling Mercies

- John 9:1; 2 Timothy 1:7; James 1:17; Proverbs; 3 John 2

32. Walking into Victory

- Hebrews 4:16; Isaiah 40:28; Proverbs 3:5-6; Philippians 4:6; Luke 10:19;
- Revelation 12:11; 2 Corinthians 2:14

33. Men Affirming Men

- Esther 4:14; 2 Corinthians 5:17; Ephesians 5:23; Proverbs 4:5; Colossians 1:27; Acts 13: 22; Revelation 12:11; John 17:17

34. Warfare Prayer

- Luke 10:18; 2 Chronicles 20:15; 1 Peter 5:7; Hebrews 12:2

35. Warfare Prayer for the Five-Fold Ministry: Apostles, Prophets, Evangelists, Pastors and Teachers

- Luke16:18, 18:1; John 9:1,10:19; Philippians 2:10,4:6; James 5:16; Psalms 91:1; Revelation 12:11

36. Warfare Prayer for Generational Controlling Spirits

- Revelation 12:11; Matthew 18:18; 2 Corinthians 10:4-5; John 10:16; Proverbs 18:22; Ecclesiastes 4:9; Romans 5:5; James 1:5

37. Warfare Prayer for Emotional Distress

- Matthew 18:18; 1 John 4:18; Isaiah 59:19; Numbers 23:19; Exodus 15:26; Colossians 1:27; Jeremiah 29:11,30:15

38. Warring Against Wrong Attitudes

- Luke 10:19, 18:1; Psalms 46:1; Ephesians 4:15,

Psalms 23:3; 119:105; 139:23; 2 Corinthians 10:4-5; Romans 12:1-2; Philippians 2:6-8

39. Warfare Prayer for Children

- Jeremiah 29:11; Revelation 12:11; Ezekiel 22:30; Luke 10:19; 1 John 2:16   Ephesians 2:8; 6: 17; Psalms 34:17, 19; 145:9

40. Prayer Against Human Trafficking

- Jeremiah 17:14; Proverbs 29:2; Psalm 103:3; 107:20; Joshua 1:6; Luke 10:19; John 3:16-17

41. Healing

- Psalms 34:10, 107:20; Proverbs 4:20-22; Isaiah 53:4-5; Romans 8:16,32; Hebrews 13:5; 3 John 2

42. Healing for Victims of Incest

- Mark 11:25; Psalms 107:20 Colossians 3:13; Revelation 12:11

43. Healing for Victims of Molestation

- Psalms 23:3, 107:20; Colossians 3:13; Mark 11:25; Hebrews 4:16; Joel 2:25; Jeremiah 30:17

44. Healing for Victims of Rape

- Hebrews 4:13; Matthew 15:27; Jeremiah 29:11, 30:17, 32:17; Philippians 4:6; Mark 11:25; Proverbs 3:24; Isaiah 26:4

45. Healing for Men who Grew up without a Father

- Isaiah 41:10; 2 Timothy 1:7; Jeremiah 30:17; Romans 8:32; Ezekiel 36:26; Colossians 3:13 John 9:1

46. Healing for those Struggling with their Sexual Identity

- Psalms 107:3; Hebrews 4:16;Genesis 1:27; John 10:19, 17:17; Jeremiah 30:17; Proverbs 18:22; Isaiah 59:19; Romans 2:4; 1 John 5:14-15

47. Healing for the Broken Heart

- Psalms 37:23, 107:20,147:3; Hebrews 13:5; Jeremiah 30:17; John 9:1, 10: 19; Isaiah 55:11;

Numbers 23:19; Colossians 1:27

48. Healing for Children Rejected by Parents

- Isaiah 53:3; Jeremiah 30:17; John 10:19 Romans 8:32; Philippians 4:6

49. Childbearing, Difficulties Conceiving, and Barrenness

- John 5:14-15; Psalms 84:1,127:3; Proverbs 30:16;Luke 10:19; 2 Corinthians 1:19-20; Romans 4:17, 8:11, Isaiah 55:11

50. Shifting the Atmosphere

- Revelation 12:11,19:16; Mark 3:15; 10:19; Matthew 6:10, 18:20, Haggai 2:9; Psalms 34:1-3; John 14:26.

51. Prayer for Israel

- Nehemiah 11:1; Zechariah 8:3; Matthew 1:1; Isaiah 62:6; 1 Corinthians 11:25; Jeremiah 32:40; Ezekiel 16:60; 1 John5:14-15

52. Peace in the Countries of the World

- 1 Chronicles 7:14; Matthew 24:6-7, 14; Mark 13:7; Isaiah 1:19, 55:12

53. Prayer for Intercessors and Prayer Warriors

- Jeremiah 33:3; Isaiah 54:17; Ephesians 3:16-21; John 10:19; Galatians 6:9; Nehemiah 8:10; Zechariah 4:6; John 15:5

THE ALPHA AND OMEGA OF PRAYER

A. Prayer- Thessalonians 5:17; 1 John 5:14-15; Luke18:1; Philippians 4:6

B. Praying God's word into Your Life- Isaiah 11:2-4; Ephesians 1:15-23; 3:14-21; Colossians 1:9-14

C. Partner with God- James 5:17

D. The Word- Isaiah 55:11

E. The Lord's Prayer- Matthew 6:9-13

F. Dressed for War- Ephesians 6:10-19

G. Love - 1 Corinthians 13:4-8

H. Wisdom- James 1:5; Proverbs 8:9

I. Joy- Nehemiah 4:8

J. Healing- Isaiah 53; Psalm 103:2-3; 34; 37; 1 Peter 2:24; 3 John 2

K. Protection- Psalm 91; 23:5; Matthew 6

L. Deliverance from Fear- Isaiah 41:10; 1Timothy 1:7

M. Favor- Psalm 5:12; Luke 2:52

N. Insight/ Foresight - Ephesians 1:15-23

O. Vision- Habakkuk 2:2-3; Proverbs 29:18

P. Financial Strategies- Deuteronomy 8:18; Philippians 4:19; 3 John 2 ; Ephesians 3:20

Q. Strength for the Journey- 46:1; Philippians 4:13; Ephesians 3:14-21

R. Courage to Stand- Joshua 1:6; Nehemiah 6:1-3; Proverbs 3:4-5; Isaiah 26:3; Hebrews 11:1,6

S. Government- 2 Chronicles 7:14; 1 Timothy 2:1-4

T. Relationships- Psalm 138-8; 1 Corinthians 13:4--8; 1 Peter 5:7

U. Prayer of Agreement- Matthew- 18:19

V. Resist the Temptation to Quit- 1 Corinthians 10:13; James 4:7

W. Faith- Mark 11:22-24

X. Marriages- Ephesians 5:22-23; Colossians 3:13

Y. Children- Psalm 127:3; Ephesians 6:1-4

Z. Your Rights In Christ- Matthew 11:28-30; Mark 1:8; Luke 10:19; John 16:23-24; Romans 8:1-2,14,17, 26, 32

About the Author

Ethlyn O. Farrell or Etty as her many friends call her is a woman of many talents. She has authored two (2) books: a devoional, *Alone in the Presence of God*, released in 2011 and a mini-book, *There's a Miracle in Your Mouth*, released in 2013. She is actively working on several other books other than this book,

Prayers That Touch Heaven and Change Earth. With deep roots in her faith, along with a strong love for God and His people, Ethlyn is committed to going to the next level in Christ, waiting with great anticipation for the next move of God.

Ethlyn is also the founder of Victory In Prayer Center, which launched on March 4, 2013. It's a prayer website, www.victoryinprayercenter.com, where individuals can post their prayerrequest(s) and testimonies to answered prayer.

Ethlyn resides on the beautiful island of St. Thomas, US Virgin Islands, surrounded and loved by eight (8) siblings and many friends. Holding onto God's unchanging hand, Ethlyn's greatest desire is to use her God-given talents to evangelize and win others to salvation.

Ethlyn Ottley Farrell

Prayers That Touch Heaven And Change Earth

www.ingramcontent.com/pod-product-compliance
Lightning Source LLC
Chambersburg PA
CBHW070628300426
44113CB00010B/1695